A home for all SEASONS

A home for all SEASONS

KAY PRESTNEY & BECCA CHERRY

RYLAND PETERS & SMALL
LONDON • NEW YORK

PHOTOGRAPHER Becca Cherry
SENIOR DESIGNER Megan Smith
EDITOR Sophie Devlin
LOCATION RESEARCH Jess Walton
CREATIVE DIRECTOR
Leslie Harrington
SENIOR COMMISSIONING EDITOR
Annabel Morgan
HEAD OF PRODUCTION
Patricia Harrington

First published in 2024 by
Ryland Peters & Small
20–21 Jockey's Fields
London WC1R 4BW
and
341 E 116th Street
New York, NY 10029

www.rylandpeters.com

10 9 8 7 6 5 4 3 2 1

ISBN 978-1-78879-612-5

A CIP record for this book is available
from the British Library.

Library of Congress CIP data has been
applied for.

Printed and bound in China

FSC www.fsc.org MIX Paper from responsible sources FSC® C106563

contents

Our Manifesto

- We believe in the emotional and physical benefits of living in alignment with the seasons.
- We love to use a seasonal palette and embrace biophilic design to live in harmony with nature.
- We feel the benefits of slowing down, creating sustainable crafts and embracing seasonal rituals that celebrate the passing of the year.
- We seek an antidote to the fast pace of life, resisting consumerism and trends.
- We take care to design a home purposefully, a timeless interior that tells your own story.
- We appreciate the beauty of simplicity, blurring the lines between indoors and out.
- We value a mindful life, following the rhythms of nature to enhance both your wellbeing and your home.

Biophilic Design

INSPIRED BY NATURE

We can connect to the seasons in our homes in a variety of ways. Houseplants, foraged foliage and seasonal flowers are a great way to bring the outside world indoors. And studies have shown that images of the natural world (photographs, paintings or prints) are highly beneficial to our wellbeing, too.

The term 'biophilia' translates as a love of nature and living things. It was coined in the mid 20th century and has since developed into a field of study that explores humanity's innate connection to nature.

The American social ecologist Professor Stephen Kellert, known as 'the godfather of biophilia', theorized that we can never be truly healthy if we are alienated from the natural environment. Kellert's 72 principles of biophilic design have found many practical applications as today's designers seek to use natural materials, colours, forms, textures, patterns, scents, sounds and imagery to create spaces that boost our physical and mental health. Many scientific studies have confirmed that we, as humans, benefit from a close connection to the natural world. When we breathe fresh air, witness the motion of waves or leaves moving in the wind, touch a natural material such as wood or stone, observe the fractal patterns in the head of a sunflower, inhale the petrichor scent of the earth after the rain or feel the warmth of the sun on our faces, we feel better. Although our world has changed radically from the days when our ancestors lived in caves, our mental functions remain similar. This means that the fast-paced, hyper-connected, highly stimulating environment in which most of us now live can be overwhelming and have a negative impact on our health and wellbeing.

The ways in which our predecessors sought calm and safety can inspire the design of our homes today. Prospect-refuge theory describes how a cave (refuge) would have had a clear view (prospect) of any predators, while providing reassurance that no danger could approach unseen from behind. Today, a similar arrangement might take the form of a window seat facing out into the garden. Similarly, the savanna hypothesis suggests that living in environments surrounded by nature combats stress and improves both our mental and physical health. Biologically, we are simply unable to thrive without feeling close to nature.

In the following pages we will share ideas and examples of how we can harness the principles of biophilic design to create that vital connection to nature and enjoy the benefits it brings us within our homes.

ÅHLÉNS
LINEN
M

A Room for All Seasons

Spring & Summer Styling

Having a seasonal home doesn't mean limiting your decor to a single season – we can adapt our living spaces to reflect the passing of the year in its entirety. These two photographs show Nat Woods' beautiful home in Sussex (see pages 70–79). In spring and summer, this living space has a fresh, minimal feel and is filled with bright green foliage, pretty flowers and lightweight linens.

Autumn & Winter Styling

In the cooler months, the same room takes on a more tactile and enveloping style. The sofas are piled with sheepskins, woolly blankets and velvet cushions, inviting you to curl up by the fire. A wooden table replaces the linen-covered ottoman and is topped with a curated display of glowing candles. Nature is present in the form of evergreen branches gathered on winter walks.

Calm, energized, relaxed or stimulated – colour can bring these sensations to life. Colour psychology teaches us how to alter the mood of our homes through the considered use of colour. It has the power to transform living areas from cold, unwelcoming spaces into warm, comforting retreats.

The colour spectrum plays a pivotal role in shaping our emotions and influencing our mood, having the potential to completely alter how we feel; each colour being tied to specific feelings (see 'Colours and their meanings', right).

While some believe that only the seven colours of the rainbow (with tints, shades and hues of each) exist, others maintain that there are more than two million unique colours that can be identified. Although there are limited names in our language for the hundreds and thousands of hues that we see around us, there is no doubt that how we choose to use them in our homes can have a powerful effect on our wellbeing.

Colours can be categorized in three different ways: warm or cool, light or dark and bright or muted. The combinations in which these qualities are used can completely alter the feel of a space.

Neutrals provide a versatile backdrop, the perfect canvas for pops of colour added in the form of furniture, textiles and accessories. However, even black, white and grey have many different shades. Each of them can be warm or cool with undertones of red, blue or yellow.

Colours can be used harmoniously in a space or be loud and disruptive. We can create a soothing sanctuary with cool tones or an uplifting haven with warm tones. Learning what makes us happy is key. Perception of colour is completely subjective based on each individual's way of seeing and personal preferences. What is energizing to one person may be overwhelming to another.

Colours and their meanings

- **RED** The most vibrant colour of the spectrum, associated with passion and energy.
- **ORANGE** Warm and energetic, orange exudes enthusiasm and positivity.
- **YELLOW** An endlessly optimistic colour – the colour of sunshine, inspiring creativity and joy.
- **GREEN** The centre of the colour spectrum and the colour of nature. Green represents perfect balance and calm. Great for relaxation and stress relief.
- **BLUE** The colour of the oceans, lakes and rivers. Blue is tranquillity and serenity. It promotes a calm and peaceful atmosphere.
- **INDIGO** A deeper, more dramatic version of blue. This is a colour that encourages intuition.
- **VIOLET** Often linked to luxury and creativity. Violet can evoke a sense of inspiration, introspection and spiritual awareness.

The changing colours of the natural world and seasonal colour palettes can inspire us in choosing colours for the home. Nature always attains perfect harmony so that each season's palette works together effortlessly, and the same effect can be achieved indoors, too.

Our homes play such a huge part in our lives. Embracing the beauty of the seasons and letting them guide our colour choices can help ensure that the places where we live become sanctuaries that aid our physical and emotional wellbeing.

Spring

Spring: a season of growth, optimism and colour. A time to let in as much of the increasing daylight as possible by cleaning windows, swapping heavy winter textiles for lighter linens and moving from inward-facing, cosy spaces to rooms that look to the outdoors. Spring homes are joyful, playful and uplifting places. They reflect the vibrant energy of the season and the sense of awakening and renewal that the return of light and warmth brings. Scandinavian houses often feature window seats and furniture that's carefully placed to enjoy the benefits of nature from inside the home until it is warm enough to throw open the doors and windows and truly blur the lines between indoor and outdoor living. Ostara, the March spring equinox, celebrates rebirth and growth, the balance of light and dark; this is a good time to plant seeds, spring-clean and bring the uplifting colours and flowers of spring into your home.

A Spring Home

Cotta (AE)
Citrine (Little Green)
Jonquil (EB)
SOFT PINK
173
MADE UP

Colours of the season

The spring palette is warm with yellow undertones; it is light, clear and bright. As the landscape gradually comes to life again after the long months of winter, its stark, bleached tones are succeeded by an abundance of lush green growth as new buds, shoots and leaves start to burst forth and unfurl. Long-awaited spring shades include the vivid, clean yellows of daffodils, mimosa, primroses and buttercups. Leafy and lime greens sit harmoniously alongside pale pinks and lilacs, reflecting this season's flowers as they emerge from green shoots.

For those who desire to fully embrace a spring home, walls are painted in joyful and uplifting colours in paler shades. Not just the preserve of children's rooms, the spring palette can be used to create playful and vibrant spaces for all ages. On a smaller scale, a tired vintage cupboard repainted in a sunny shade of pale yellow, a grass-green flatweave rug, a couple of lilac linen cushions added to the sofa or simply a glass vase of freshly cut spring flowers on the kitchen table will all bring the positivity of spring into your home.

Textures & materials

Spring patterns and materials reflect the light, bright and optimistic spirit of the season: ditsy floral prints, cottons and loosely woven linens and playful polka dots all sit well in a spring home. Mixing freshly picked flowers from the garden such as muscari, alliums, daffodils, bluebells and hyacinths with vibrant green houseplants in a variety of shapes, tones and leaf textures will bring a soft yet energizing feel to living spaces.

Take a leaf from artist Philippa Jeffrey's creative spring home (see pages 36–45) and use sample pots in seasonal shades to add pops of light, fresh colour and pattern to your home. Try adding a simple painted runner to a plain wooden staircase, revive an old picture frame with pastel polka dots or breathe new life into a vintage piece of furniture with some hand-painted flowers.

Collect spring fabrics and wallpapers to create a mood board for the season that will provide inspiration for decorating ideas, or frame a beautiful piece of patterned wallpaper or hand-stitched fabric to hang in a corner for a shot of spring. Colourful accessories in glass, wicker, ceramic, stone and enamelware all offer an opportunity to bring this most hopeful of seasons indoors.

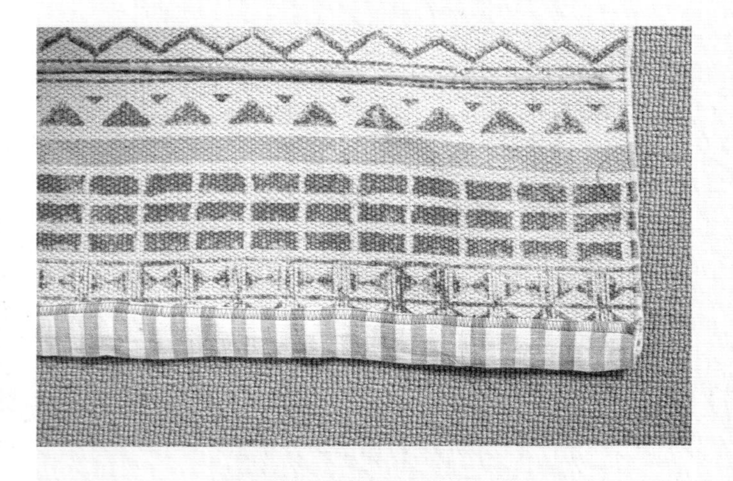

PAINS
clean la cuisine naturelle
Les basiques chocolat
La pâtisserie
LE CUISINIER EN CANDIDAT LIBRE

Designing with nature

Getting outside to enjoy the lighter days and recalibrate our circadian rhythms in the spring sunshine offers an opportunity for gathering natural finds and bringing them home. From statuesque magnolia branches to diminutive primroses, add seasonal interest by welcoming the outside in. Large vases filled with stems of blossom, mimosa, lilac or cow parsley bring welcome colour and scent into our homes and echo the abundance of the natural world as it awakens from winter. Use galvanized buckets, old milk churns or glass demijohns to display large branches (weigh down the bottoms with sand or stones if they threaten to topple over), and highlight the jewel-like charms of delicate spring flowers such as lily of the valley or violets by arranging them in a cluster of ceramic or glass vases; mix heights and textures for added interest.

Use the colours, patterns and forms of the natural world to decorate – think of a pretty botanical wallpaper, a floral fabric or gingham café curtains offering privacy at a window while still letting in the light.

A NEW BEGINNING

Deep in the wild Charente countryside of south-west France, Isabelle Dubois-Dumée and her family have swapped a busy Parisian lifestyle for a fairytale existence in their 12th-century château. The vibrant spring greens and soft earthy tones of the rural landscape form the basis of Isabelle's design scheme in which nature and texture abound. Natural materials, local flora and tactile vintage pieces create interest, each room a layered visual delight.

SPRING GREENS
Simple arrangements of seasonal flowers and foliage are dotted throughout the house (this page). The green doors are painted in Les Portes du Château, a colour created by Isabelle with paint brand Ressource based on the original paintwork found in the castle (opposite).

In 2015, Isabelle, her husband Hubert Bettan and their three daughters Augustine, 24, Lilou, 22, and Pimprenette, 20, spent a family holiday near the pretty town of Angoulême in the Nouvelle-Aquitaine region. 'We were happily settled in Paris, but something stirred inside us that summer: a sense of freedom, a desire for new experiences, the lure of the untamed countryside. Interested in the local history and property, we took a spontaneous trip to a castle for sale,' Isabelle explains. The visit turned out to be a life-defining moment. The whole family fell in love with the idea of a new adventure, living at a slower pace in tune with nature while bringing the run-down château back to life as their new home. 'Our friends didn't believe us when we returned to Paris to share the news that we had bought a castle and were moving to the Charente!' says Isabelle with a laugh.

Built from the white limestone typical of the region, the castle was originally constructed as a defensive fortress with four towers, a moat and a drawbridge. When Isabelle and her family arrived, the towers were uninhabitable, the main building was severely dilapidated and the roof was in a state of total disrepair.

Style Tip

In the kitchen, stacks of wooden crates provide open storage for ceramics and glassware, cooking ingredients and tableware. 'I like to be able to see things, to appreciate them and to use them frequently,' says Isabelle. These displays are interspersed with trailing plants and seasonal flowers gathered on her daily walks in the meadows and woodlands.

'It was incredibly exciting and utterly overwhelming,' says Isabelle. 'We had so many ideas, but a limited budget and so many things that needed attention.'

She and Hubert are concentrating on enjoying the restoration journey, making this special place habitable room by room. They have embraced its imperfections and created a simple, natural interior in contrast to the imposing architecture. 'Nature is my guiding thread, my signature. I use wood, rattan, ceramics, linens and stone to create interiors that blend seamlessly with the landscape beyond.'

An artist, set designer, stylist, photographer and owner of interiors brand Les Petites Emplettes, Isabelle uses her many creative talents to bring together spaces that appeal to all the senses and are both calming and intriguing. Each room at Château de Dirac has its own personality, but also integrates harmoniously into the whole. White walls offer a gallery-like backdrop for her chosen pieces, creations and foraged finds that fill the castle.

Isabelle has used her signature green paint throughout to highlight the beautiful oversized doors, architraves and skirting/baseboards. 'I love to use green in my interiors – it is a constant reminder of spring, the magic of rebirth and the way the countryside bursts with a thousand shades.'

A huge fan of vintage and secondhand shopping, Isabelle particularly enjoys collecting ceramics and old French linens. 'I prefer that they don't all match, but I stick to my colour scheme of earthy tones, fresh greens and neutrals to retain a sense of visual calm,' she explains.

STAY GROUNDED

Original bird-motif tiles have been preserved in the kitchen – images of nature in our homes offer a calming presence and similar benefits to being outdoors (top). The work surface was made with planks of wood from the forest and the splashback is simple plywood (above). Wooden crates are stacked with a flat desktop to make a useful workspace in a terracotta-tiled corner (opposite).

PLENTY
DANS MA CUISINE
VÉGÉTARIENNE

NATURAL COMFORT
Layered raw materials have been used to create a cosy living room. Round woven pouffes sit on a large jute rug encircling a homemade wooden coffee table. A corner sofa made with crates and wooden planks is topped with an array of differently sized cushions in many shades of green.

Isabelle also spends time in Morocco where her mother has a property in the Marrakech medina – a rich source of the many baskets, rugs and pieces that add texture and comfort to her interiors. 'I am deeply inspired by the crafts of Morocco and have forged great connections with many of the artisans there who have created pieces for me, which I now sell in my interiors shop,' she shares.

Another trademark of Isabelle's style is the wooden crates that she cleverly stacks to create bespoke storage – long shelving for linens, bedside tables/nightstands filled with books and floor-to-ceiling displays of ceramics and glass in the kitchen and hallway. The latter are interspersed with seasonal plants and flowers, which are allowed to age and dry. 'I walk daily in our meadows and woodlands and always return home with armfuls of grasses, seedheads, branches, leaves or stones, which become part of the decor, connecting us to our surroundings and the changing seasons,' she says.

The property may be a vast château, but it retains a homely feel thanks to Isabelle's creative design ideas, which are grounded in simplicity. Curtain poles have been fashioned from branches or garden canes, while the long linen drapes hang from metal clips or are tied with garden string. Everyday items are often repurposed: upstairs, a length of bamboo garden screening has been attached to the wall creating a headboard; old linen sheets are used as bedspreads or to curtain off shelving under a bathroom sink.

With so much of their budget needing to be spent on costly projects such as restoring the roof, the couple have made many pieces of furniture themselves, creating the 'pebble' dining table using wood found on site and sets of trestles, the surrounding chairs an eclectic mix of secondhand finds. The kitchen island has been made with more of Isabelle's wooden storage boxes, topped with sanded wooden planks. Underfoot, restored original wooden floorboards are exposed and layered with simple jute rugs in different shapes and sizes to zone large spaces, adding comfort and texture. Downstairs, original floor tiles help to keep the house cool in the heat of the summer.

EMBRACING IMPERFECTION

Adhering to an earthy palette brings visual calm to a collection of ceramics (left). Peeling paints and crumbling plaster are retained and celebrated for their patina (above). A display of birdhouses draws the eye to the curved staircase (opposite). Plants on the floor and walls bring nature indoors.

Lighting a large house can be expensive, but Isabelle has artfully strung long rows of affordable rattan or white festoon fairy lights across the rooms. At night they cast a soft glow and bring a party atmosphere to the castle. Large rattan pendants make a statement in the kitchen, while inexpensive big paper ball shades have been used upstairs. Over the dining table, an intricate artwork of hundreds of glued wooden skewers forms a light shade that floats like a cloud above the table, casting interesting shadows.

A natural collector, Isabelle is constantly adding to the castle rooms in an organic design process influenced by serendipitous finds and creativity rather than trend-led or manufactured style. 'I find it difficult to turn off my mind – I see inspiration in everything. I hope my style is natural and beautiful, simple yet refined and joyful. I love to create interesting interiors that draw people in to discover the details,' she explains. She advocates buying items you love even if they may not immediately have a place, seeking out unusual and secondhand finds and allowing time and thought to give them a new lease of life.

The couple are rewilding the castle meadows and have created a large vegetable garden where they grow their own food, enjoying the opportunity to eat seasonally that this brings. As they slowly but surely breathe new life into more rooms, Isabelle continues to adhere to her style mantra: 'I've always tried to make my interior blend with the exterior. To bring the harmony and calm of the outside world indoors using the rhythm and materials of nature as my guide.'

ALL IS CALM

Isabelle's design recipe of wood, natural grasses and white linens runs throughout the castle. A branch from the garden fills a bedroom corner and is used to hang rattan festoon lights above the bed (opposite). In the bathroom, plants are suspended from the ceiling in tactile woven baskets (above). Woollen and quilted throws add colour and texture to the bedroom – you can always store useful and attractive items in plain sight if you don't have built-in cupboards (above right). A sheer bedroom curtain made from old linens filters the strong sunlight (right).

THE ART OF LIVING

'Spring is my favourite time of year – I love to watch the countryside come to life and the sense of hope and a fresh start that it brings,' says artist Philippa Jeffrey. 'Using the colours of this season throughout our home gives me a daily sense of joy.' Philippa's 18th-century stone cottage in Oxfordshire acts as an extension of her beautiful canvases, where soft pastel colours and creative details abound.

PLAYFUL PATTERN

Philippa's home is a riot of pattern and colour that avoids overwhelm by keeping to a soft spring palette (above). Seasonal flowers in old glass bottles frame a pretty-covered vintage book (above right). Lush greenery fills the house in both physical and pattern form (opposite).

Philippa's home is a masterclass in creating unique and characterful interiors using artistic tricks that elevate the ordinary to the beautiful. Hand-painted stair runners were created using tester pots, and small samples of high-end fabrics have been sewn to the edges of shop-bought cotton rugs: a clever way to bring expensive designer material into a home at low cost.

Describing herself as 'an artist, mother and treasure hunter', Philippa always has a project on the go. She has created a joyful home using a spring palette of pinks and greens inspired by the textures and colours of the natural world. When she and her family decided to move out of London, the Grade II listed property was the first house she viewed and it was love at first sight. 'Although it felt huge with its three storeys and six bedrooms, it was a cosy warren rather than an imposing house, which I loved,' she recalls. The layout was perfect for family life, with plenty of rooms for work, rest and play.

THE ART OF NEEDLE CRAFT

NECK
CHUCK
RIB
LOIN
PLATE
FLANK

Two spaces in particular had instant appeal. 'The kitchen with its lofty ceiling and mezzanine had great wow factor and was a space where we could hold big gatherings. And there was a huge barn that I could imagine as a beautiful artist's studio and gallery for my work.'

With a previous career history in the magazine world, Philippa has always been drawn to the printed word. Her many books and periodicals collected over the years have become part of the decoration in carefully curated displays.

PRETTY IN PINK

Philippa put her own stamp on the kitchen cabinets by painting them in Cuisse de Nymphe Emue by Edward Bulmer (opposite). The tiled splashback adds eye-catching pattern. A trio of statement rattan lampshades draws the eye to the high ceiling (above). A mix of vintage chairs around the table lends an informal feel.

Seasonal Decor

NATURAL DYED EGGS

For a fun spring craft, pierce a small hole at either end of a fresh egg and blow gently through the top, pushing the contents out into a bowl underneath. Repeat for the rest of the eggs, then carefully rinse the shells and leave to dry. Loop a small piece of thin wire into each egg and tie a piece of string or ribbon to the top. Bring pans of water to the boil and make your natural dyes: turmeric for yellow, red cabbage for blue, spinach for green, red onion skins for lilac and beetroot for pink. Add 1tbsp vinegar to fix the dye and put the eggs in the water for 4–24 hours, depending on how deep you want the colour. Set aside to dry completely before adding a pretty painted pattern.

EAT, DRINK, PAINT

The spacious kitchen had instant appeal for Philippa, who loves to cook for family and friends (opposite). The table also serves as a space for family crafting and painting sessions and a canvas for Philippa's seasonal tablescapes. Her artistic skills are evident throughout the house, for instance in the hand-painted sage green stair runner (far right).

Piles of back issues fill the inglenook fireplace, while books with pretty covers are framed or propped as pieces of art. Foraged finds and upcycled pieces discovered in local vintage shops sit alongside handmade family creations, artworks and new items that have caught Philippa's eye. Art is a family passion and her children Freddie, 10, and Maggie, eight, both love to produce pieces to decorate their home. The colourful canvas that hangs high above the kitchen stove is one of Philippa's artworks, with the children's collages added for a fun and personal piece that is a much-cherished family treasure. It is a great talking point for the many friends and family who enjoy Philippa's cooking at gatherings around the kitchen table that go on into the small hours.

Philippa took time to work her way through the house, first future-proofing with roof and window repairs before she allowed herself to let loose with her paintbrush. Using a mix of paints and wallpapers, a neutral backdrop mixed with statement patterns allows Philippa to curate each room over time. 'I love to visit antiques shops, junk yards and quirky independent shops where I often pick up interesting new pieces to add to our home,' she says.

Style Tip

Choose a favourite colour to run as a thread throughout the house – greens appear here in patterns, plants, paints and fabrics. Take inspiration from Philippa's love of vintage, too. A wooden bookcase frames a green-and-white botanical wallpaper (top left) and an old lamp base has been painted white and given a fresh new shade (above right).

Most items, old or new, that cross the threshold are given the 'Philippa treatment', whether it is painting her trademark stripes onto a plain picture frame, using beautiful art papers as a backdrop to interesting prints or painting pieces of secondhand furniture to give them a new lease of life. 'My style ethos is eclectic – I love to mix and match and am a firm believer that more is more. And I try to add my own touch to things so that our home will always be unique and personal to us.'

Spring florals and botanicals play a big part in Philippa's home – in material, printed and painted form. No room is without the thread of green that runs through the house.

GLOBAL STYLE

Philippa has gathered design influences from her travels and worked them into her interiors. Pattern and colour abound in the bathroom and children's bedroom (opposite). Indian bone-inlaid furniture and block-printed textiles sit among calming white linens in the master bedroom (this page). An antique frame lends one of Philippa's own canvases a vintage feel.

Houseplants also play a major role in bringing nature and colour into the interior. Large statement structural plants in tactile wicker baskets add a sense of scale to the vast kitchen, while in less spacious rooms small plants are displayed in an array of pots and vessels. Philippa also loves to gather flowers and foliage from the garden and her walks in the surrounding fields to display, press or dry for year-round interest. Yet, whatever the time of year, there is always a feeling of spring in this home.

SPRING COLOUR

The seasonal palette continues outdoors, where a vibrant euphorbia pops against the Cotswold stone (above). On the stone patio, the kitchen doors are flung open as the weather warms and life spills out into the garden once again (right).

A door for all Seasons

With doors feeling a little bare once Christmas wreaths have been taken down, we can look to the historic French tradition of leaving an anonymous *brin de muguet* (lily of the valley) posy on a friend or neighbour's door to celebrate May Day and bring good luck. Whether it is a few flowers left in secret, or an abundant floral handmade wreath, spring flowers are perfect for bringing a shot of colour and joy to your door. Here, we have created a vibrant seasonal wreath using the sunshine yellow of mimosa flowers with some cut branches of pussy willow for added texture.

WHAT YOU NEED

A base wreath (we used a shop-bought one made from twisted willow, or you can create your own from grapevine cuttings, weeping silver birch branches or clematis vine), a selection of spring flowers and flowering branches (look for woody stems to make it easier to push them into the wreath), pruning shears and a length of spring-coloured ribbon.

1 Lay the wreath base on a flat surface and prep the foliage and flowers. Cut pieces measuring 20–25cm/7¾–10in in length, leaving a clear stem of 7–10cm/2¾–4in. Leave some flowering branches 10–15cm/4–6in longer for a wilder feel. Arrange the stems around the edge of the wreath to get an idea of how many you will need.

2 Start pushing your shorter stems into the wreath at a 45-degree angle, working clockwise around the edge. Slightly overlap each one as you go to keep the wreath looking plentiful. Hold it up and make sure all the stems are securely tucked in and the wreath base is evenly covered.

3 Add in your longer branches at intervals around the edge. Don't be too uniform about this – try to imitate the wildness of nature by keeping your composition irregular. When you have finished, hold your wreath against the door and secure it with your ribbon at the desired height.

Thinking ahead

* Prepare for the warmer days of summer when you will enjoy sitting outside. Give old garden furniture a clean and a lick of paint, or search a vintage emporium to find a colourful bistro set to brighten your outdoor space.

* If you have a glasshouse, now is the time to take everything out, clean and sort the contents ready for spring planting. See if there is space for an old wooden chair in a corner for days when it is not quite warm enough to sit outside. If you don't have a glasshouse, consider covering an old table with zinc sheeting to create a planting bench instead.

* Sort through all your seed packets. Group them into vegetables, annuals and perennials and plan where they will go in your garden. Plant seeds in flowerpots, eggshells, empty yoghurt pots and cans, or make your own pots out of newspaper. Place them on a sunny windowsill and wait for the green shoots to appear!

Summer

After the high energy of spring, summer brings a slower, more languid pace of life with sun-bleached materials, lightweight fabrics and soft, light interiors. Days are at their longest: the solstice, also known as Litha, celebrates the abundance of nature and the lure of lakes, rivers and oceans. We are drawn to the outdoors, to the light and warmth that summer brings. Indoors, we embrace sheer fabrics, big florals and open windows. Summer is heavily scented: roses and sweet peas, honeysuckle and jasmine. As night falls, fragrant herbs and nicotiana plants release sweet aromas into the evening air. Moving furniture and accessories outdoors, we can create alfresco spaces in which to enjoy the comforts of home with the freedom of being out in nature. An inviting armchair under a tree, a picnic blanket at the beach, a dining table in the garden... here we can pause, daydream and rest.

A Summer Home

Colours of the season

The summer palette is muted and has a softness and delicacy – a faded version of its vibrant spring counterpart. Its colours are drawn from the cooler end of the spectrum, with blue-grey undertones. They are calming and soothing, romantic and restful. Think of aquamarine seas, blowsy roses in a summer flower garden and gentle pastoral landscapes. Weathered off-whites are reminiscent of sand dunes, bleached grasses, late summer fields of corn and straw baskets. Perennials and annuals jostle for position in the flower beds, a riot of pinks and greens.

Summer interiors tend to emulate the style of beach huts and cabins. Off-white walls form a backdrop to this season's big florals, whether the armfuls of hydrangeas or peonies on display or the patterns that flow across wallpapers, curtains and bed linens. Cool blues echo the refreshing water that we seek on hot days – streams and ponds, lakes and rivers, seas and oceans. Soft blues can be found in summer flowers: nigella, cornflowers, sea holly and sweet peas. We can bring these muted tones into the summer home through textiles, painted furniture and linen tablecloths.

Textures & materials

Whether or not we are able to enjoy a holiday in the sun, we can still bring a feeling of midsummer into our homes. Materials are tactile and natural: wickers and rattan, cottons and silks. Layering our homes in the same way that we layer our clothing allows us to adapt to changing temperatures throughout the day.

Bleached, limed or whitewashed wood can be used for floors, walls or furniture. Vertical cladding will draw the eye upward in smaller rooms, whereas horizontal planks can help widen a narrow space.

Woven baskets may be kept piled up ready for summer adventures, adding texture and perfectly embodying the William Morris adage: 'Have nothing in your house that you do not know to be useful, or believe to be beautiful.'

Linen or muslin curtains reduce the glare of the hot sun, filtering the light and keeping interiors cool. Hung high and pooled on the floor, they add softness and their gentle ripple in the summer breeze brings a calming sensation. Patterns of this season are stripes and ticking, chintzy florals, checks and ginghams. Antique lace and broderie anglaise conjure the romance and softness of summer.

Designing with nature

Bringing the big flowers of summer into our homes adds scent, colour, texture and joy to life indoors. Large hydrangea heads in glass vessels, cut roses tumbling out of stone vases and potted geraniums lining windowsills fill the house with the abundance of summer.

The season also has a delicate side: the smaller blooms of daisies, strawflowers, cosmos and nigella alongside the tiny fragile flowers in a cloud of gypsophila. Translated into interiors, we see ditsy floral prints alongside big floral wallpapers, printed or embroidered throws and cushions covered in large-scale blooms.

Pressing flowers is a fun and creative way to capture the season. Use them to make floral artwork in vintage frames, or look for old botanical books in charity/thrift shops and create a gallery wall of floral prints.

Collections of shells and pebbles in glass vessels (such as attractive jars or interesting vintage pieces) are a tactile and engaging addition to a tabletop or shelf that preserve the memories of summers by the sea.

WOODWARM
Maxime
PASSY

NORTHERN LIGHT

This traditional sunshine-yellow home in the heart of the Swedish countryside is filled with flowers, whether freshly picked from the cutting garden or in the abundance of pretty floral fabrics and wallpapers that fills the rooms. It is a creative family home that moves with the seasons, but truly comes into its own in the summer months when the big garden glasshouse and rose-covered veranda become part of the living space.

A HANDMADE HOMESTEAD

A simple wooden fence protects Veronica's flower garden (this page). The couple built their glasshouse by hand, filling it with vintage furniture from local shops (opposite). Terracotta pots of geraniums on the refectory table pick up the texture of the reclaimed brick flooring.

Home to chef and interior designer Veronica Lindmark, her partner Richard and their two children Carl, eight, and Ingrid, six, this large wood-clad property is also shared with Richard's mother. This harmonious arrangement benefits all three generations and reflects the family's historical ties to the century-old house. It was previously owned by the Swedish steel manufacturer SSAB, where Richard's father worked; he rented it as part of an employee housing scheme until the 1980s, when he was able to purchase it as a permanent home. 'It is lovely to be able to recreate childhood memories with our own children and share with them stories of the past, while adding new ones of our own in this special home,' says Veronica.

Veronica spends her working week creating inventive dishes and expressing her creativity through seasonal produce and delicious flavours, but at the weekends she turns these skills to her other passions: interior design and flower growing. At home her ingredients are paint pots, floral wallpapers and carefully curated textiles, which she has brought together using a muted summery palette in shades of green and blush pink.

The result is a serene family home that is both functional and beautiful. She continues to honour the hand-crafted origins of the house: each addition is carefully considered and timeless rather than led by trends.

Limewashed walls and soft, natural textiles in gentle shades are the blank canvas for Veronica's decorative schemes. She loves to seek out pretty artisanal wallpapers, keeping collections of these rolled up in baskets and shelving units around the house that have become displays in their own right. In daughter Ingrid's bedroom, a patterned wallpaper of cream-coloured hares and leaves on a mossy green background is playful yet calming. And in Carl's room, Veronica has juxtaposed a bold floral wallpaper in soft greens and pinks with a more delicate design of green leaves and white star-like flowers on the opposite wall. A cork pinboard propped on the desk is covered with leaves painted to look like foxes and ghosts – one of the many nature-based creative projects Veronica enjoys with her children.

The couple have added narrow tongue-and-groove cladding to many of the rooms in their part of the house, a design trick that draws the eye upward to give the illusion of height in small spaces. Borrowing from another hand-crafted

SUMMER STYLE

Veronica has captured the gentle warmth of the season using dusky pinks, soft blues and olive greens, with plenty of white as a calm neutral. Layered textiles in these colours help create a romantic and tactile feel in the living room (left). In the kitchen, an old table has been painted white and now serves as an island (above right). A curtain hides open shelving and potted plants highlight Veronica's love of floral details. Her treasured collection of ceramics is artfully displayed in a painted dresser/hutch with glazed doors (below right).

tradition, they have hung Shaker-style hooks high on the walls to provide additional storage for everyday clothing, accessories and foraged finds. A bunch of dried strawflowers hangs on wooden pegs in the dining room alongside a vintage wicker basket, ready to be filled with craft materials for the next project.

Veronica is an avid fan of local auctions where she enjoys finding unique pieces to transform into something beautiful for her home. 'I paint a lot of furniture, sometimes using the same colour as the wall and at other times choosing a soft green or pink to gently contrast,' she explains.

'I like to buy large free-standing pieces that are both useful and attractive – for instance, I use glass-fronted cabinets to display my collections of porcelain, glassware and fabrics.' She also enjoys regular trips to the flea market, seeking out interesting treasures. 'My style is a characterful blend of old and new. The common thread is always calming hues, timeless pieces and hand-crafted finds that spark conversations and also encourage relaxation.'

Unsurprisingly for a chef, the heart of this home is the kitchen. Although long-term plans are afoot to enlarge and update the space, Veronica has proven that you don't need a big showroom kitchen to cook and share great food. Plain white cabinets and a white wood floor make the most of the natural light, and a vintage table has been upcycled into a useful kitchen island with additional storage and prep space. Simple linen curtains shade the glare of bright sunlight in the summer and conceal items stored on open shelves, reducing the visual clutter and softening the small space. The little dining room also works hard. 'It is my favourite room in the house because of its cosy and inviting feel,' says Veronica with a smile. 'I love gathering friends and family around the handmade dining table, which I set with my favourite porcelain and always fresh flowers from the garden.' In the warmer months, the doors are flung open to the wooden veranda, letting in a summer breeze that carries the heady scent of the rambling roses. Out here, a wide cane chair layered with comfortable textiles is an idyllic spot in which to relax and enjoy the rural setting.

ON DISPLAY

In the master bedroom, a selection of cushions in muted checks, stripes and florals adorns the bed and a vintage artwork above picks out the same shades (opposite). Veronica has a large collection of pretty dresses and clothing, which she displays on Shaker-style hooks in the bedrooms, carefully curating each rail to suit the feel of the space. Pastel-hued and floral-patterned dresses bring a summery feel to the master bedroom (below and below right), while a more autumnal collection waits for cooler months in a guest room (right).

CHILD'S PLAY

For the children's bedrooms, Veronica has chosen timeless wallpapers and patterns that will age with them (this page and opposite). Creative vignettes add interest to every surface and yet, thanks to the limited palette, the rooms retain a sense of calm. Little dens carefully built into the design encourage imaginative play. Floor space, desk areas, soft play zones and places to display their favourite finds and creative makes are all included.

Style Tip

The garden glasshouse is filled with Veronica's seasonal blooms. Follow her trick of keeping an eye out for interesting glass vessels in secondhand shops or save attractive food jars. These can then be filled with pretty flowers and displayed in groups along windowsills or hung from thin wire and curated with each season.

The large garden is where Veronica feels at peace, whether she is growing vegetables or flowers for cutting. The large glasshouse fulfils a multitude of roles all year round. 'We love hosting parties and suppers out here – watching the sunset and eating under the glow of candles and festoon lights feels magical,' she says. Handmade touches abound, from the display cupboard built by Richard to the terracotta lampshades made by Veronica. Prize blooms from the cutting garden fill an array of vintage glassware and old bottles. In spring the walls are lined with geranium cuttings, which grow into a floral display that fills both the glasshouse and the main house in the summer and early autumn.

Living seasonally is important to Veronica, who gains a sense of wellbeing and balance from existing in harmony with the beautiful Swedish countryside. 'I love to bring things into our home that reflect the uniqueness of the different times of the year, to spend as much time as possible in nature and to be surrounded by flowers at all times,' she says. 'I hope our home fosters an awareness of the environment in our children as we appreciate the beauty and significance of nature in our lives.'

Seasonal Decor

TERRACOTTA CLAY LAMPSHADES

Try Veronica's clever craft project using air-drying terracotta clay to make organic-shaped lampshades to hang in your home or garden room. Roll out the clay and mould it by hand, cutting out a circle in the centre for the light fitting, then leave to harden. If the space has no electrical power, use a rechargeable camping bulb.

DAIRY TALES

Where the counties of Hampshire and West Sussex meet, a pretty cottage known as The Dairy House is home to Nat and Dug Woods. Reclaimed materials sit alongside French antique finds in this rustic-luxe house, its sun-bleached interiors created on a tight budget with hard work, vision and creative flair.

Built from brick with wooden shiplap cladding, the three-bedroom house sits nestled in the shadow of a large 17th-century thatched threshing barn. Unusually for a 30-year-old property, it has a Grade II listing from English Heritage, meant to ensure that any development is aligned with the adjacent historic building. 'We were taken aback to discover that our relatively modern house was listed and it has definitely made our renovation journey longer, but it has also ensured that we have created a timeless home in keeping with its surroundings,' says Nat.

CAREFULLY CLAD

Painted shiplap and an abundance of flowers give the home's exterior a rustic feel that belies its age (above and above right). Within, wide planks have been used throughout to elongate the rooms (right). Those on the floors have been limed, while the planks on the walls have been painted white.

PASSY GRIGNY

Style Tip

Add calm interest to a space with a minimal palette of neutral shades. Paint window frames a shade or two darker than the walls for a subtle contrast. Mixing natural materials such as wood, ceramics, stone and metals creates a tactile and inviting feel that encourages touch and stimulates the senses.

OPEN HOUSE

To increase the feeling of space, Nat has used open shelving rather than wall cabinets (above). Aged brass is used as an accent metal to bring together the shelf brackets and drawer handles.

The couple previously lived in a terraced house on a busy estate in Hampshire, but they yearned to move to the countryside, having both enjoyed a rural upbringing. 'We had planned to save for another two years before moving, but I happened to see this property online and coaxed Dug into a viewing,' Nat explains. 'We fell for the beautiful location, the summer-holiday feel of the shiplap, the large garden and the potential for extending the house. Just 24 hours later we had found a buyer for our home and The Dairy House was ours!'

Although the sale happened quickly, it has been a long journey to create the beautiful home they enjoy today. The house needed new cladding, electrics and a heating system. 'When we moved in 13 years ago, we had no budget – it was four years before we could afford to do anything, and even then we did a lot of it ourselves,' Nat recalls. In the end, the building had to be completely gutted and extended. The three original rooms downstairs were opened up to make a light-filled, open-plan space with a new double-height living room at the rear. Nat loves to mix old and new and has worked hard to ensure that the new interiors are filled with character and texture. She has brought in reclaimed floorboards, wooden panelling and architectural salvage pieces such as a set of old shutters, which has been cleverly repurposed as a room divider between the snug and dining room.

All the rooms have carefully styled vignettes, little visual stories put together by Nat to remind her of travels, conjure a moment in time or evoke a particular feeling. 'I love treasure hunting and antiques – for me, nothing beats the thrill of a beautiful and unique find. I have lots of pieces collected over many years and love to display them in our home.' Creating decorative displays of shells, sea urchins and pebbles brings a feeling of summertime into the interior, whatever the season. Stoneware pots filled with daises are dotted throughout the house and left to dry as summer moves into autumn.

Nat loves to collect ceramics, which she displays in softly coloured antique French display cabinets sourced from her favourite vintage sales: the local Ardingly Antiques Fair in West Sussex and The Country Brocante, a travelling fair established by Lucy Haywood. In the kitchen Nat has made wooden shelving, painted to match the walls, where aesthetically pleasing collections of bowls are piled ready for use. Nearby a row of handmade mugs, all differently patterned, hangs from a copper rail beneath a beautiful framed canvas. 'I have a lot of things, but I avoid clutter by sticking to a neutral palette of chalky, muddy colours to retain a sense of calm,' she explains.

A CURATOR'S EYE

A carved wooden shelf on the wall houses a textured collection of seashore finds (above left). Hand-thrown mugs hang from a brass rail in the kitchen under a beautiful still-life painting, all echoing the bleached summer hues that run throughout the house (above).

WEATHERED WOOD

The neatly painted wall cladding contrasts with the uneven, aged patina of a vintage wooden china cabinet that houses more collected ceramics (this page). An old painted canvas propped on top adds a burst of colour and evokes coastal memories.

Nat has echoed the external wooden cladding inside the cottage using wood sourced from The Reclaimed Flooring Co. Underfoot, limewashed floorboards are tactile and comfortable. She has also used planks on the walls: in the new snug extension they are painted white, their vertical lines drawing the eye up to the apex beamed ceiling and giving the space a New England feel. Upstairs, whitewashed planks form headboards with little sills where thoughtfully curated pieces bring interest and texture to the guest bedroom. One of her treasured finds, a wooden vintage apothecary unit with delicate original labels, offers great storage and a visual statement in the master bedroom. Vintage botanical prints in soft tones have been framed and hung in groups around the house, another way to bring nature indoors. In darker corners of the house Nat has hung decorative vintage French mirrors to reflect the daylight and brighten the room, having whitewashed their frames to blend them into the decor.

In summer the garden becomes part of their living space. Textured hazel fencing provides privacy around a scaffold-board deck. Here, under the shade of the large cedar tree, the couple enjoy alfresco dining throughout the warmer months. 'I leave the front door open and treat the garden as an extension of our home,' says Nat. 'We plan to build a barbecue/grill area for summer entertaining. We have learned to grow our own veg, too – we now invest much more time into living seasonally.'

A COASTAL FEEL

The master bedroom is home to a striking vintage apothecary cabinet (opposite). Blue-and-white ticking and a little wooden boat bring in nautical elements (left). An armchair in the kitchen takes advantage of a sunny spot under the window (above). A collection of summer fishing and shopping baskets hangs on the bedroom door, ready for impromptu picnics (below).

The garden has an English cottage garden feel, mixing evergreens for year-round interest with perennial planting and seasonal bulbs. Old zinc containers have been repurposed as planters, which can be moved to fill any seasonal gaps in the borders. Nat has made sure to include her favourite plants: 'I love foxgloves and planted them so that I could bring them indoors in spring and early summer as cut flowers. I also grow rowan, hydrangeas, white alliums and salvias, which can all be used in arrangements to enjoy in our house as well as in the garden.'

The cottage may look finished, but Nat will always have an idea percolating. 'Our house is constantly evolving to meet our changing needs, and I don't think that will ever end,' she says. 'I'm currently dreaming of adding a shepherd's hut!'

Seasonal Decor

FLORAL NAPKIN RINGS

Woven willow napkin rings have been given a summery touch by attaching tiny flowers with floristry wire for a pretty addition to the dining table. Look for varieties with small flower heads that dry well, have strong stems and won't wilt in the heat. Strawflowers, sea lavender, gypsophila and wax flowers all work well.

ALFRESCO DINING

Nat and Dug have built a raised deck under the shade of the monkey puzzle tree to enjoy summer meals outdoors (top left and opposite). Smaller potted plants such as thyme and hydrangeas can be easily placed on the table for decoration, scent and colour. Vintage French grain sacks have been made into large bolster cushions for the woven chairs (right). The surrounding flowers have been carefully chosen for both their appeal in the garden and for cutting (above).

MOTHER OF PEARL &
TRADITIONAL
HARDWARE
MERCHANTS
TRADING
New Star
FILTER

LESSONS IN LIFE

An old Swedish schoolhouse is now home to photographer and stylist Mari Magnusson and her husband Finn. Its lofty classrooms are filled with carefully curated props that Mari uses in her work. The decor is Scandi rustic with a neutral backdrop that allows the many vintage pieces to shine. Life here is creative and relaxed, lines between indoors and outdoors are blurred and days often finish with a wild swim in the nearby lake.

SLOW LIVING

Mari loves to spend time curating displays using foraged and found items (opposite). A newly established cutting garden provides abundant summer roses with their delicate form and scent (above left). Time spent at the local lake brings Mari peace of mind and a connection to nature (above).

Built in 1897, the property served as the village school until the mid 20th century, when it became an assembly hall for the nearby church. 'I love that so many people have happy memories of our home – weddings and baptisms have all been celebrated here,' says Mari. 'Although, we still have the original naughty corner in one of the old classrooms, so perhaps not everyone remembers being here so fondly!'

The Magnussons have three children of their own: Milo, 20, Misha, 18, and Noah, 11. They previously lived in England and Australia and continue to spend time in Finn's native France. The white walls are typical Scandi minimalism, in keeping with Mari's roots, but French brocante finds, English vintage pieces and Australian treasures are all to be found in her artfully styled displays. 'Our whole house has been furnished from thrift and vintage stores all over the world,' says Mari. 'I brought a lot of pieces with me from our former homes in London and Melbourne, and I mix them with new accessories from my favourite Swedish shops such as Granit and H&M Home.' Large vintage cupboards have been painted and used to house Mari's vast collection of ceramics and textiles, which she has built up over the years. Foraged seasonal finds are woven into the displays and a hanging branch in the master bedroom serves as an aesthetically pleasing hanging space for Mari's choice pieces of clothing.

Here in the countryside of central Sweden, the family enjoys living a rural life, but the major cities of Stockholm, Uppsala and Västerås are all conveniently situated within an hour's drive. Mari and Finn both work from home, so the house works hard as an office and photographic studio. 'I often create content for brands, so the house is very much a constantly changing canvas – I really enjoy swapping things round and changing the way it is styled to suit the job I am working on,' says Mari. 'It also gives me a great excuse to collect lots of wonderful finds, which become my props.' The large windows were also a big draw when viewing the house, as each room is bathed in plentiful natural light; a photographer's dream.

The four-bedroom house is spacious and inviting, but in the summer the family spends as much time as possible out in the garden. With a footprint of 6,000 square metres/ 64,580 square feet, it has been divided into adaptable living spaces by fences, hedges, arbours and pergolas. At its heart is a beautiful white-painted wooden glasshouse with a brick floor, which houses a long refectory-style table and benches where the family dines in the warmer months. Mari has created a rustic metal chandelier with candles that can be lit at night to accompany the festoon lights with their cosy glow. Additional outdoor rooms filled with old pieces of furniture have been styled to offer a quiet place to read or work under the sky.

STYLIST AT WORK

Mari has amassed a large collection of props, gathered across continents, for her styling and photography work. Artfully stored using an array of cabinets, shelves and surfaces in every room, they draw you in for a closer look (opposite). Above Mari's long trestle desk, a classic Anglepoise wall light illuminates a mix of monochrome finds (right). A corner of the photographic studio has been given a summer style-up with pretty pastel cushions and posies of flowers from the cutting garden (below).

ALL THE WHITES

In the kitchen, armfuls of freshly cut summer hydrangeas sit in the old Belfast sink, ready to decorate the house (above left). A vintage white wall cabinet houses ceramics and glassware (above). Mari paints many of her vintage pieces in varying shades of white so that they blend into the background of her shoots, allowing her to easily change the feel of a space, either with her clients' products or with colourful accessories (left).

CUPBOARD LOVE

A large vintage cabinet, painted deep grey with a white interior, houses more of Mari's extensive props collection (right). The items on display reflect the colours of nature – greens, earthy browns and whites. Dried flower heads, stacked ceramic bowls and a colour-toning matchbox form an attractive vignette (below).

In the cutting garden, Mari grows favourite flowers such as roses, peonies, gypsophila, dahlias, hydrangeas and pretty grasses to use in her styling work. The vegetable garden is also thriving, allowing the family to be self-sufficient during the summer months with the help of seasonal workers from abroad. 'We host students from around the world who come and work here in return for food and lodgings – in the evenings we play board games together and learn about each other's cultures,' Mari explains.

A lot of work has gone into thoughtfully restoring this historic home, including several big projects such as replacing the heating system, repairing the old roof and restoring the wooden façade of the house to its former glory.

Style Tip

If you have large collections of things, try grouping them by colour to avoid a feeling of clutter. Juxtaposing different textures such as glass, ceramic, stone and wood is more visually interesting than storing all your glassware together. Place objects with different heights and shapes alongside one another to encourage the eye to move through the collection.

The original floorboards have been sanded and the walls coated in chalk paint from Jotun or Kalklitir for a textured and breathable artisanal finish. With lots of interesting architectural features including traditional wooden cladding and ceilings that are up to 3.5 metres/ 11½ feet high, the colour palette is kept light and neutral to maintain a feeling of calm and space.

Mari also enjoys decorating the house according to the season. In winter she makes pine wreaths and brings in small trees and branches from the nearby woodland to add colour and texture, but she enjoys the warmer months most of all. 'Summer is my favourite time, when I can bring plants from my glasshouse into our home and line the windowsills and tables with potted geraniums or cut flowers,' she says. 'The days are long and the house and garden merge into one airy living space.'

BRANCHING OUT

Bringing nature indoors bestows a sense of calm. Bare twigs hung with paper Christmas ornaments have been left in a corner for year-round interest, while a large cut branch in a sculptural vase brings wow factor to the bedroom (this page). Driftwood suspended with rope serves as additional hanging space for clothes (opposite).

GARDEN STYLE

Mari's attention to detail and love of curated collections extends into her garden. A grouping of flowering potted plants on a vintage wooden table welcomes visitors to the entrance of the beautiful glasshouse, which is hidden within the cutting garden (above). Metal plant stands and arches are placed throughout the garden, creating height and interest and leading visitors into the next in a series of enchanting outdoor rooms (right).

FLOWER POWER

Shelves of scented geraniums line the walls of the glasshouse and are often taken into the main house for decoration (right). A long wooden table doubles as a dining table and floristry workspace where Mari arranges flowers from the garden (below). A vintage shelving unit is used to store and display potting tools and an array of interesting vases. Roses grow in abundance all over the garden, with longevity through the summer and into late autumn (below right).

A door for all Seasons

This romantic doorway captures the natural beauty of summer, creating a joyful floral welcome for visitors and those returning home. Seasonal foliage and softly coloured summer blooms weaving around a sky-blue door add texture and interest to the whitewashed brick façade of a country cottage. Whether you want to add an unexpected touch of whimsy for a summer party, spruce up a tired doorway or just add a little seasonal joy to your home, the steps below will show you how to recreate this pretty summer door.

WHAT YOU NEED

Wire cutters, chicken wire, floristry wire, a hammer, three strong nails, pruning shears and an array of summer flowers and foliage that will dry well and not wilt in the heat – we used hydrangeas, dahlias, eucalyptus and willow.

1 Cut two 70cm/27½in lengths of chicken wire. Roll each one up into a sausage shape and secure with floristry wire – be careful, as it is sharp. Hammer in the nails around the door at the three corners of your design and attach the chicken wire, with one length placed horizontally above the door and the other vertically to one side.

2 Tuck the foliage into the chicken wire, pushing it tightly into the middle and at different angles. Keep going until the chicken wire is completely covered. Mix the lengths and types of foliage to make it more interesting and keep the placement irregular for a natural feel.

3 Tuck in the flower heads at intervals – grouping in odd numbers looks better than even spacing. Stand back to see how it looks from a distance and fill any gaps that you see. If you have some flowering pots, put them on either side of the door for added flower power.

Thinking ahead

* An abundance in the hedgerows beckons us into the countryside for long walks to forage the fruits of the season. Gather wild blackberries and freeze for tasty smoothies and tarts as well as natural dyeing projects. Enjoy a day out at a fruit farm picking summer berries for picnics – preserve some so that you can enjoy the goodness of local fruit out of season in the winter months.

* Collect strawflowers and alliums from the garden, stringing them up to dry in cool spaces away from direct sunlight. For tips and inspiration on creating ever-lasting floral displays, follow Bex Partridge (@botanical_tales) on Instagram.

* While the days are still long and warm, now is the time to get out your autumn woollens to wash and dry ready for when the nights begin to draw in once again. There is a chill in the air around the late summer campfire and warmer layers are already being put to use.

Autumn

The autumn home is warm and inviting, somewhere to cosy up after bracing walks through the falling leaves. We are still enjoying the outdoors, but with warm clothes and around the bonfire. Mornings are crisp, with a chill to the air. The scented flowers and big blooms that have filled our homes are replaced by dried seedheads and branches of golden leaves. Reflecting the mellow palette of this season, autumn homes are softly coloured in russets, ochres and pinks. Think bare plaster walls, terracotta tiled floors and layers of warm textiles with soft blankets, woollen rugs and velvet cushions replacing summer linens. As we reach for a warm sweater, a woolly hat and a thick scarf to keep us toasty outside, so too our homes are wrapped up with additional layers. Candles offer a mesmerizing glow as the evenings start to draw in. You may want to try making your own out of beeswax or soy and scenting them with essential oils, using vintage cups and old stoneware as vessels.

Harris

Colours of the season

Autumn's palette is warm, with golden-yellow undertones. Dark and muted, it has a soft, nostalgic glow. The slow pace of summer is replaced with a renewed energy, which brings a spectacular autumn display as green leaves turn to shades of russet, amber and ochre, enveloping the landscape in a rich and earthy palette.

The deeper colours of this season are full of intensity and drama, but these striking reds, burgundy and plums are also accompanied in the autumn spectrum by mellow shades of gold, pinks and terracotta. These are soothing tones that draw us to sit around a fire, whether under the stars in early autumn or indoors as winter approaches.

Bring autumnal colour into your home with warm, inviting soft furnishings and textiles. Add cosy throws, blankets or pillows in shades of rust, amber and mustard to a bed, sofa or armchair. You can also enhance the feeling of warmth through lighting, adding lamps or candles in amber or coppery tones to create a glowing atmosphere that is reminiscent of the autumn landscape outside.

Textures & materials

Natural materials in earthy colours play a big role in the autumn home: warm woods, richly coloured clay tiles, mellow Cotswold stone and raw plaster. In contrast to the light cotton rugs of a summer home, autumn houses have wool, jute, sisal or hemp floor coverings that are snug and tactile underfoot. Mix up patterns, sizes and styles for added impact, placing a round sisal mat under a chair and using a large rectangular kilim to ground a dining table.

Wooden furniture is warmer than the bleached, limed woods of summer. Mellow-hued vintage pieces and aged painted furniture sit alongside dark wood antiques, cross-sawn timber and weathered, rusty metals. Textiles are tactile: think of an ochre herringbone throw, a Herdwick sheepskin or a bouclé armchair.

Dried flowers fill the autumn home as the abundance of summer slows and we seek inspiration and interest from silhouettes and texture. Hand-woven baskets connect us to nature and add to the tactility of an autumn home. They have a multitude of uses, too, from gathering seasonal fruits to storing quilts and blankets. Ceramics in different glazes, colours and finishes can be displayed and filled with foraged finds for extra seasonal appeal.

Designing with nature

Bringing nature into the autumn home is all about shape and form. Look to the garden for structural branches, twigs, berries, interesting seedheads and dried flowers such as poppy heads, honesty, smoke bush, allium heads or hops. Don't ignore the vegetable patch, where you can find beautiful dried forms such as artichoke flowers.

Get creative weaving dried strawflowers and bracken into a winter wreath for your door (see pages 132–133). Baskets and bowls of freshly picked seasonal fruits can be stored in plain sight, bringing colour into the kitchen while they wait to be turned into tasty crumbles and jams.

Painterly autumnal landscapes propped on a shelf, dried flowers hanging on the wall and beeswax candles on ceramic saucers are all ways to bring nature into our homes. For those still seeking the romance of fresh blooms, there are dahlias, chrysanthemums and asters for joyful seasonal colour. Leave them to dry in their vase and save the heads for wreaths, gift toppers or small everlasting posies in bud vases.

TRUE ROMANCE

In the English Cotswolds, Ali Allen's creative and bohemian home sits in the liminal space between the pretty florals of summer and the rich, tactile palette of autumn. It is filled with vintage finds, treasures from global adventures, foraged pieces, family memories and handmade items.

BOHEMIAN BLOOMS
Ali uses natural, romantic displays of flowers from her garden throughout the house (above left and opposite). Seasonal blooms tumble over vintage china vases, their colours echoing the palette of the interior. The old, mellow stone walls of the house are covered in vibrant Virginia creeper (above).

This Georgian house is home to a family of creatives. Ali is an artist and photographer who was previously an interiors stylist – this comes as no surprise, as each room is exquisitely styled and filled with painterly vignettes. Her three sons have inherited her creative flair: Barnaby is a chef at the much-loved Giffords Circus, Bertie is a maths genius and Wilfred is a fine artist and bass guitarist.

The oldest parts of this historic home date back to the 18th century. Yew trees, planted for protection, stand watch in each corner of the site. For Ali, the symbolism was particularly resonant. 'Fate drew me here after many tough years in London as a widowed single mother,' she explains. 'Walking along the lane one day, I peered over the gate and dreamed of living in such a beautiful house. A month later, the estate agent called to tell me that it was on the market.' As soon as she arrived, she knew she had made the right choice. 'The first night I spent here, I could see the sun in one window and the moon in another. I knew this was where I belong, and it has offered great solace and healing ever since.'

A handsome porch with patterned floor tiles sets the scene as you enter the house. From the stone-flagged hallway, painted panelled doors open into a series of rooms filled with charming vintage treasures. Ali's decorating style is a bohemian blend made up of layered natural textures.

Bloom

Style Tip

Ali loves to source vintage pieces that add to the character of her historic home. Emulate her style by looking out for period finds at big antiques fairs. Combine painted chests of drawers/dressers with upholstered pieces in faded florals, layered with pretty cushions for a soft, bohemian and romantic style.

MUTED TEXTURE

This is a tactile home – everywhere the eye rests, it will find variations of texture (opposite and this page). These range from embroidery and trims on striking lampshades to organic ceramic vessels filled with autumnal seedheads. Bare wooden tables celebrate the beauty of the natural grain, while a Louis XVI chair is adorned with ornate golden plaster detailing.

The gentle palette mirrors the warm tones of early autumn. 'I love to buy French antiques and market finds, and am often to be found rummaging in a reclamation yard or scrolling eBay for pieces that have patina and history,' Ali says. 'I like my home to feel tranquil and to be a calm haven from the busy world beyond.'

One of Ali's favourite indoor spaces is the sitting room, where original sash windows frame views of the garden and allow the family to witness the changing colours and textures of the natural world with each season. Sunlight pours in, bouncing off the pale pink plaster walls and the rich ochre velvet curtains to create a soft and cocooning space. Rugs and carefully placed furnishings establish zones for dining, reading and lounging throughout the room.

On every available surface, interesting collections of artefacts, beautiful objects, books, floral displays and photographs draw the eye. A wood-burning stove sits in the fireplace with its decorative carved surround. Above the mantel, an inset oval mirror reflects natural light or the flickering flames of candles into the darker corners of the room.

In the colder months, the family moves between the warmth of the sitting room and the equally cosy kitchen. Here, the old stone fireplace houses an Aga backed with decorative tiles. The organic textures of the honey-coloured Cotswold stone walls and flagged floor alongside wooden tables and chairs offer tactile, rustic charm. Materials are simple and honest – an old stone sink sits on top of an upcycled wooden console table as an alternative to a fitted kitchen. Open shelves are filled with Ali's ceramics, glass jars of dried herbal teas and garden seedheads. Off the kitchen, a large rear entrance room has huge cupboards that hold Ali's enviable collection of props for food and interiors shoots. An old round wooden table has been given a new lease of life with blue-painted legs. Walls are dotted with collections of foraged dried foliage and seedheads.

MIXED MEDIA

Ali contrasts warm woods and soft linens with tougher materials such as raw stone and silvery metals (opposite above). A fluted tin lampshade hangs above the kitchen table and engraved Moroccan tumblers hold knives and forks in a stone alcove next to the Aga (opposite below and this page).

Seasonal Decor

DRIED FLOWERS & FOLIAGE

Seek inspiration from the multitude of textures found in the autumn landscape to bring seasonal interest into your home. The fading flowers, seedheads, branches and leaves found in gardens, fields and hedgerows at this time of year make beautiful, wild bouquets that remind us to slow down alongside nature.

CURATED PASTIMES

Turn your hobbies into decorative items and display the things that bring you creative joy: painted canvases propped on a vintage cupboard, a guitar waiting to be played and carefully sourced vintage pieces hung as *objets d'art*.

Upstairs, Ali has created a peaceful sanctuary in the master bedroom. The eye is drawn to plentiful vignettes of meaningful items around the vintage bed: dried flowers, propped artworks and a collection of crystals, all chosen to induce a feeling of centred calm. In the en-suite bathroom, an old wooden table with a propped mirror and small basin form a pleasingly rustic vanity unit on the herringbone brick floor. A cast-iron claw-foot bathtub placed under the sash window allows bathers to gaze into the forest beyond.

Ali has recently discovered a passion for fine-art floral photography, and often finds inspiration in the bountiful garden where she grows flowers, herbs and vegetables. Brick, stone and gravel pathways meander through a series of outdoor rooms planted with fruit trees, perennial beds, vegetable patches and rambling roses. 'I love my garden – it is like a living, breathing painting and there is no better place to really feel the seasons,' she says. 'I am slowly changing the planting, introducing medicinal herbs and cutting flowers. I would live in the garden if I could.'

Hidden away in the garden is a beautiful glazed orangery, where Ali has set up a painting and claywork studio as a haven far away from the digital world. An old wooden refectory

BROCANTE STYLE

In the bathroom, an ornate chandelier is suspended above the tub, while a simple fisherman's lantern lights the vanity (opposite). Foxed mirrors and aged brass taps/faucets give a softer feel than modern designs. Painted canvases propped on a radiator echo the floral abundance outdoors (this page).

table fills the room and life drawings by Ali are propped against the old plaster walls alongside dried seedheads collected from the garden. Tubes of paint and pottery tools sit among plants and dried flowers. A trio of off-white clay pendants made by Ali hangs over the table, their organic forms offering a warm light as dusk falls.

Just like the garden, Ali's house is a constantly evolving canvas. 'My favourite room changes daily according to my mood. I like to keep a sense of fluidity by moving items around, allowing things to come together that feel harmonious and in keeping with the season.' Nature provides continual inspiration for her photography, painting and claywork, too. 'I bring in flowers and branches all year round.'

This is a home where life slows and its inhabitants are deeply connected to the natural world. Ali has recently begun studying quantum botanical energy healing, a branch of alternative medicine based on flower essences and essential oils. 'Living seasonally is absolutely necessary to my wellbeing. I adore autumn with its misty mornings leading into the subtle, soft golden light of the afternoons – these things never fail to make my heart sing. I find the gradual letting go during the quiet stillness of autumn very inspiring. It is always a very creative time for me.'

A CRAFTED HOME

Traditional Victorian features meet design influences from Scandinavia and Japan in Laura and Andy Logan's timeless London home. Craftsmanship, simplicity and the celebration of natural materials lie at the heart of this soulful abode.

Home to Laura, Andy and their children Bonnie, five, and Alban, two, this five-bedroom property in east London is a celebration of materials and workmanship. The original stone, brick and timber structure dates back to 1867, when it was the first house to be built on this street. Laura, an interior designer, has used a blend of contemporary and traditional materials including limewash paints, wooden joinery and Forcrete microcement to create a calm and timeless family home. Layered textiles made of natural linen, cotton, wool and grasses soften the hard surfaces, while wooden floors and limewashed walls create a tactile environment that feels peaceful and inviting.

SOMETHING OLD, SOMETHING NEW

In the kitchen, new handmade ceramics sit alongside vintage stone vases and seasonal foliage on a wooden shelf (above). Laura has mixed bespoke modern cabinets with timeworn vintage pieces such as a weathered old refectory table, which has been repurposed as a kitchen island (right).

TREEHOUSE LIVING

An architectural branch stands out against the serene limewashed and microcement surfaces of the dining space (opposite). Its appearance reflects the changing seasons. In autumn, drying leaves are silhouetted against the walls. The artwork is by Alexandra Yan Wong and the Moroccan vase on the table is from A New Tribe.

Originally from Yorkshire, Laura was attracted to this area for its sense of community. She and Andy had bought and renovated a smaller house nearby, but their family had outgrown the space and they were looking for a new project. 'I would often walk past this house and always felt drawn to its dimensions and period character,' Laura remembers. 'Since childhood I have been fascinated by the idea of houses as repositories of people's stories and this felt like the perfect place in which to write a chapter or two.'

The couple carried out major renovation works, adding a kitchen extension and removing internal walls to open up the downstairs floor. 'I loved the Victorian frontage, but the interior layout was confused and there was a disconnect between the garden and the living spaces.

Style Tip

Custom-designed, built-in cabinetry allows every corner of a living space to be used. Display treasured handmade ceramics on open shelves and in glass-fronted cupboards, where they can be enjoyed when not in use (above). A window seat offers a place to enjoy nature with its garden view. Curating a shelf of unusual objects counters the uniformity of a row of kitchen cabinets (left).

I wanted to create a light-filled, open-plan interior where cooking, playing, relaxing and socializing could flow seamlessly through the house and out into the garden in the warmer months,' Laura explains. Working with Bristol-based architect Lizzie O'Neill of E J Studio, the couple chose a glazed oak-framed extension with large doors that open to blur the lines between indoor and outdoor living. This became an early focal point that led the design process. 'I wanted to prioritize the idea of functional fluidity and flow as a core element of the design, while emphasizing local craftsmanship and natural materials throughout,' says Laura.

Influenced by the design ethos and traditions of Japan and the Nordic countries, Laura has created an organic and tactile home where simplicity, form and function reign. She loves to commission pieces from local makers, including pottery from PPP Lab, Ditte Blohm, Sway Ceramics and Clare Spindler and a wooden stool from Sally Graveling Studio. Statement objects are used in vignettes that draw the eye with their unusual shapes and finishes. Nothing sits gathering dust, everything has a purpose and even special pieces are used often. Laura also enjoys participating in the design process and seeing her ideas come to life. For instance, the ceramic pendants hanging in the kitchen were made by local potter Hannah Stacey to her design.

SHAPE YOUR STYLE

Laura has cleverly repeated a continuing rectangular form throughout this space. The Shaker-style doors of a built-in storage cupboard align with the panelled Victorian shutters in the tall bay window (above left and opposite). A Balinese-style rattan-fronted cabinet continues the theme (left). Despite the eclectic global mix, a calm visual continuity is maintained through colour and shape.

AN AUTUMNAL PALETTE

Laura has brought the colours of the season into the master bedroom: russet and oat-hued linens, warm brass wall lights and a geometric artwork by Lucy Naughton (left). Earthy-hued ceramics are displayed on a String shelving unit devised in the 1940s by Swedish designers Nisse and Kajsa Strinning.

Laura also loves to source interesting vintage pieces to add character to the space. 'I am committed to using natural materials and repurposing objects,' she says. 'One of my favourite items is the old refectory table, which has been through the wars but is such a cherished part of our home. Each mark is a story rather than an imperfection.'

Light and texture also play a big role in Laura's designs, as she seeks to bring the sunshine indoors throughout the seasons and uses materials that bounce and reflect daylight around the rooms. 'A very special place in the house is the dining alcove – there's something magical about the way the limewash plays with light here, creating depth on an otherwise plain wall and forming a cocoon where you can sit and look out at the garden,' she says. 'I'm a huge fan of the lime paint made by Bauwerk Colour. Not only does it look incredibly beautiful on the walls but it is natural and breathable – good for us and the environment.'

Biophilic design is another core element of Laura's interior design work; she is a firm believer that incorporating nature into our homes contributes to our wellbeing and overall health. 'I love to keep a large branch from the garden in the vintage urn in our dining alcove and change it with the seasons to reflect the changes in the natural world.' The display evolves from budding tree blossom in spring and abundant leafy greens in summer, to desiccated richly coloured leaves in autumn and bare branches with interesting silhouettes in the winter months. Laura also adds scent in the form of natural candles and essential oils diffused through the house to create another sensory element. This allows her to change the feel of the interior environment from uplifting eucalyptus to earthy, woody blends that are both calming and grounding.

This is a home that works throughout the seasons, but has autumn at its core – the earthy materials and palette, the abundance of bare wood and golden light. It is a haven in which life slows and simple joys are appreciated. This time of year is a treasured season for Laura: 'Autumn is always a time for recalibration. The earth slows down, velvet dawns and dusks become ever more part of our waking lives and we embrace the changing pace and face of nature in our home.'

SPA STYLE

Laura has drawn on Moroccan influences to create enveloping, calm spaces in which to wash and bathe. Opalescent zellige wall tiles bounce sunlight around the family bathroom, while wooden shelving and rows of hooks provide storage without the need for cabinetry (above left and above). Trailing plants bring nature into the room. Downstairs, a small cloakroom has a wall-mounted sink that maximizes floor space (left). Installing brass taps/faucets directly on the walls is another space-saving trick.

settle

INTO THE WOODS

As you drive through the trees along leaf-covered tracks, the pressures and overwhelm of modern life fall away. A stay at Settle Norfolk brings back the simplicity and joy of living in alignment with the seasons. This unique collection of cabins and old train carriages hidden in the forest nurtures a close connection to the natural world. Inside each one, owners Jo and John Morfoot have set the scene for the perfect autumnal escape.

Decades of family history tie Jo and John to the land at Settle. It was bought by John's late father Peter in the mid 1970s to create a haven for wildlife, where nature lovers could spend time outdoors and under canvas. Peter also set up the family business Morways Reclamation, which John, sharing his father's passion for giving old pieces new life, continues to run today.

The cabins at Settle contain clues to the pathways that have led Jo here: selling vintage garden brocante finds, flower growing and floral design. Guests are welcomed with artfully curated displays of seasonal local flowers and foliage, housed in vintage containers. Locally raised, Jo travelled the world teaching floral workshops and retreats before returning to the land of her roots.

TAKE A SEAT
Welcoming corners can be found everywhere at Settle, beckoning guests to sit and soak up the beauty of their surroundings. A vintage leather armchair offers fireside warmth (opposite) and each cabin has a veranda with outdoor seating (this page). Potted plants are grouped on a bistro table, another of Jo's thoughtful touches.

WORKING WITH WOOD

Timber surfaces create an enveloping natural interior in the cabins. Reclaimed doors separate the bathroom from the kitchen, where a vintage cupboard provides attractive storage (left). Cleverly designed seating with built-in storage made with reclaimed wood combines form and function in the living space (below). The cosy wood-burning stove sits atop stored firewood from the Settle forest. Cabin beds make great use of the space and layers of comfy bedding draw you in as night falls (opposite).

The initial plan was to offer boutique stays in converted shepherd's huts, but John envisaged something more unusual that could accommodate a double bed and a separate bathroom. When he was offered an old train carriage for the reclamation yard, he realized it was the perfect solution. He sourced a second carriage and, after careful and considered renovation work, Settle opened in spring 2019.

The carriages, of which there are now three, were originally goods wagons. Jo and John have worked hard to preserve the character and materials throughout the renovation process, choosing to display proudly the markings and patina of their past. Many of the items found within have been sourced from Morways, adding another layer of history through tactile pieces that have their own tales to tell. Interesting pieces of embossed industrial hardware are used as handles for clever custom-designed carpentry made from beautifully coloured reclaimed wood. The built-in seating and cabin beds are combined with a thoughtful edit of vintage chairs, tables and accessories.

Meanwhile, Jo has used her talent for interior design to seek out new rustic-luxe textiles and decorative pieces in natural materials, including softly coloured linen curtains, snug throws for the beds and specially commissioned handmade ceramics for the kitchens. The style of the cabins has been such a hit with guests that Jo has created an on-site woodland shop housed in a bespoke pavilion made of reclaimed wood, where visitors can buy many of these items to take the feel of Settle home with them.

Style Tip

Bring some Settle autumnal style into your home with pretty seasonal floral displays – try richly coloured chrysanthemums in pots and freshly cut dahlias in interesting vintage containers (right). Layer up cosy textiles on beds, armchairs and sofas: think woolly blankets, fluffy sheepskins and quilted throws alongside plenty of pillows. Look out for vintage furniture that can have different uses – an old wooden milking stool could have a new life as a side table, a step stool or a plant stand.

All the wares are carefully sourced from small businesses and makers with sound ethical and environmental practices. The range includes carved wooden spoons and accessories by Steven Mackus, hand-thrown stoneware mugs by Nathalie Hammond and woven textiles by Amy Spires.

A feast for all the senses, the cabins have been carefully curated to offer a beautiful and luxurious yet rustic and soulful escape. 'We want our guests to feel realigned and rested after a stay at Settle, having spent time reconnecting with both themselves and the natural world,' explains Jo.

A ROOM WITH A VIEW
All the windows at Settle look out into the forest or to the lake (above). The colours of the leaves are a changing canvas that can be enjoyed from every room.

Heavily influenced by the beautiful rural surroundings and the Norfolk landscape that changes with each phase of the year, Jo loves to embrace seasonal living. 'On crisp winter days we gather friends to cook in the Settle field kitchen, and then we wrap up warm to sow the first seeds in the glasshouse come early spring,' she says. 'In high summer we enjoy impromptu wild swims in the lake, and as autumn arrives, we forage for berries and foliage to cook and to decorate with.'

This is the season that truly holds Jo's heart. 'Autumn is the most spectacular time of the year; it lends itself to simple pleasures such as walking Settle's parkland and witnessing the glow of turning leaves.' She continues: 'I adore the rich palette and slanted, golden sunlight. The pace of life is slower and I love to spend time over the stove tending slow-cooked, hearty casseroles with deep seasonal flavours.'

In the cabins and carriages, antique radiators and wood-burning stoves keep guests toasty indoors, while firepits and outdoor kitchens enable visitors to enjoy the great outdoors throughout the year. Settle offers abundant inspiration for rustic-luxe natural interiors and a life lived in close connection to nature. It is a place where time slows and you can wander and dream. For those who dream of running away to the circus, an exciting arrival is coming soon. Jo and John are currently renovating a showman's wagon with a stunning copper-clad roof, which will sit alongside the other cabins hidden away in the calm of Settle's woodland.

CRAFTED WITH CARE

Each cabin is equipped with a thoughtfully curated collection of locally made wood and ceramic tableware, with a few vintage pieces as well (opposite). Using these items encourages slow living – each mouthful is savoured, its vessel admired. Enamelware and wooden chopping boards bring rustic style (right). A vintage wooden table has been cut down to create a cosy dining space (below). The wooden cladding continues onto the ceilings for a cocoon-like feel (below right).

A door for all Seasons

Making a wreath is a lovely way to immortalise a special walk in a favourite place, or the landscape of somewhere that holds a place in your heart. It is a visual daily reminder of joyful memories. Wrap up and head outside with a basket and some pruning shears to find tactile, pretty dried foliage, grasses and flowers. When you get home, have fun weaving the colours and textures of autumn into an everlasting design for your door. You could also add a variety of foraged finds such as feathers, interesting twigs or pine cones for texture.

WHAT YOU NEED

A shop-bought wreath base (or make your own with twisted branches and floristry wire), strong scissors or pruning shears, plenty of seasonal foliage, dried flowers, twigs and seedheads, a hammer, a nail and a length of ribbon.

1 Lay your wreath base, whether ready-made or hand-crafted, flat on a tabletop. Cut your seasonal foliage, dried flowers and seedheads ready to tuck into the wreath. Vary the lengths, colours and textures of the cut stems and branches to make your arrangement more interesting.

2 Begin tucking the cut lengths into the wreath base, working clockwise from a 3 o'clock position and placing the foliage at a roughly 45-degree angle. Try to intersperse different colours and play with texture and shape, avoiding uniformity for a natural, wilder wreath.

3 Look at the wreath as a whole, adding in more pieces where needed. We made a full wreath, but you can try leaving a third or more of the base exposed for an alternative style. Attach a nail to your door and hang up the finished wreath using a piece of ribbon in an attractive autumnal colour.

OW TO MAKE COFFEE

Thinking ahead

✶ Plant a summer-flowering climber around your door for colour and scent next year. Try star jasmine for fragrant and pretty flowers with evergreen foliage, Chilean potato vine for sweet-smelling flowers and autumn fruit (inedible, but decorative) or traditional English climbing roses for their romance and scent.

✶ Hang seedheads and late-flowering plants to dry for everlasting use in creative projects and displays around your home. Hydrangeas, alliums, poppies, scabious, strawflowers and honesty all work well. Save the seeds to plant for future harvest.

✶ Plant bulbs now for spring and summer colour next year – daffodils, hyacinths and crocus bulbs should go into the ground in early autumn, followed a month later by hardy summer bulbs such as crocosmia, lilies and alliums, then tulips last of all. Plant narcissi in bowls and vases, then hide them under the bed until midwinter for festive, scented displays.

Winter

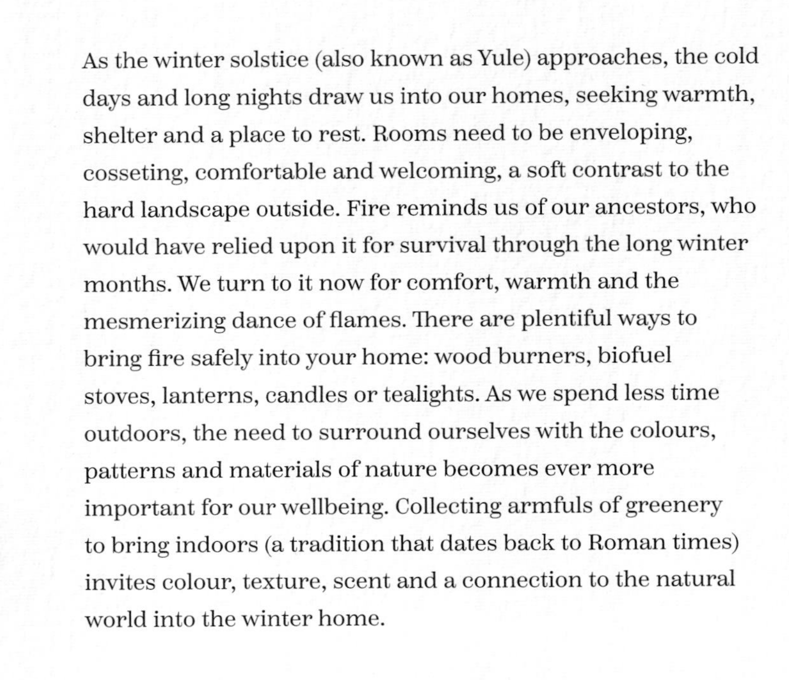

As the winter solstice (also known as Yule) approaches, the cold days and long nights draw us into our homes, seeking warmth, shelter and a place to rest. Rooms need to be enveloping, cosseting, comfortable and welcoming, a soft contrast to the hard landscape outside. Fire reminds us of our ancestors, who would have relied upon it for survival through the long winter months. We turn to it now for comfort, warmth and the mesmerizing dance of flames. There are plentiful ways to bring fire safely into your home: wood burners, biofuel stoves, lanterns, candles or tealights. As we spend less time outdoors, the need to surround ourselves with the colours, patterns and materials of nature becomes ever more important for our wellbeing. Collecting armfuls of greenery to bring indoors (a tradition that dates back to Roman times) invites colour, texture, scent and a connection to the natural world into the winter home.

A Winter Home

Colours of the season

From the warmth of autumn, winter's palette transitions back into cooler colours. Darker hues with blue undertones reflect the winter landscape as it embraces a serene calm and nature's deep hibernation begins. Deep reds are seen in the berries of holly, rosehips, hawthorn and rowan. The dark greens of pines, bay, rosemary, cedar and holly stand out amid the silhouetted branches of the deciduous trees in a cool, bare countryside.

Neutrals also play a big part in the winter palette with the off-whites of snowy landscapes, early snowdrops, heavy winter skies and the arrival of hellebores, cyclamen and camellias. In our homes, we can bring out cosy sheepskins, textured cushions, posies of winter flowers and pale candles.

Outside, the natural world is a tableau of striking contrasts. There is an air of mystery and an ethereal quality to winter that is both haunting and enchanting. A thread of autumnal warmth can be sewn into winter decor, the dusky pink of early sunsets and late sunrises that offsets cooler tones.

Thoughtful blending of these colours will create a sanctuary that mirrors the tranquil beauty of winter while enveloping you in a cocoon of warmth.

Textures & materials

You can embrace the textures of winter by bringing in pine cones or evergreen branches to infuse rooms with the earthy essence of the season. Add warmth with thick blankets, velvet cushions and tactile sheepskins, which invite you to sink into their soft embrace on chilly evenings.

The patterns of winter are checks, tartans and a festive stripe reminiscent of candy canes. Get creative with paper, crafting folded seasonal decorations, paper snowflakes and paperchains to decorate your home. Large Japanese-style snowy white lanterns are a great, affordable way to bring a gentle light to a room. Experiment with scale – an oversized orb in a small space makes a playful statement.

The many colours and textures of wood are found throughout the winter home: think of logs piled high by the fire, scrubbed wooden tables and rough carved bowls filled with pine cones. Save the ends of used candles to melt down and pour over the cones to make your own natural firelighters.

Seedheads and dried flower heads remain as bounty from autumn, with new forms appearing as the landscape continues its winter hibernation.

Designing with nature

Deck the halls with evergreen foliage and continue throughout the house – ivy, bay, holly, rosemary and eucalyptus may be used to decorate a mantel or woven through the bannisters of a staircase. Use seasonal foliage to draw attention to architectural details such as old beams or a ceiling rose.

Large branches can be wrapped with fairy lights and propped to light a dark corner, or hung from the ceiling to draw the eye upward and add a cosy glow.

Look out for vintage green glass bottles or demijohns to fill with branches laden with berries or pine needles, bringing the reds and greens of the winter landscape into your home.

Sweet-smelling narcissi bulbs planted and tucked away in autumn can be brought out and forced into winter flowering by displaying them in warm rooms, which will encourage their blooms.

Weave a winter wreath to hang outside as a welcome to visitors (see pages 162–163), or bring the textures and colours of the season indoors. For an ethereal effect, try twisting together lengths of *Clematis vitalba*, also known as old man's beard.

HMT
ASTURIAS

EVERGREEN HEARTH

An old medieval hall house surrounded by asparagus fields in the south Norfolk countryside has been lovingly renovated using vintage and reclaimed finds to create a soulful family home where imperfections are celebrated. The pace of life is slow and, in winter, it is the perfect place to hunker down by the fire with a good book, wrapped in cosy blankets.

Beautiful and historic Tanyard Farmhouse is home to Jen and Tom Harrison-Bunning and their daughters – Blythe, four, and Sorrel, two – as well as Tarka the whippet and Kipper the cat. The oldest parts of the property date back over 800 years. It is a house grounded in its surroundings that has evolved over the centuries using natural local materials, with a timber frame, wattle-and-daub walls and a thatched roof. Pantiled outbuildings were added in the early 19th century and now house the kitchen, the scullery and Tom's photography studio.

A CURATED HOME

Thoughtful vignettes include an old wall-mounted wooden box filled with vintage ceramics (above). Antique urns and jugs/pitchers house dried flowers and foliage that tone in with the muted interior winter palette of the house (right).

Style Tip

Mix materials for a pleasingly sensory home (this page and opposite). Jen and Tom have brought together a worn leather armchair, metal school chairs, a weathered wooden trough and a painted chest of drawers/dresser. Their decor celebrates the original textures of the wooden beams, limed walls and tiled floors.

Tom is a commercial photographer and Jen is head of digital for magazine and book publisher Slightly Foxed. The couple previously lived in a light and airy Victorian flat in south London, but were outgrowing their space. 'We came to view Tanyard on a midsummer's day and saw the fields of asparagus fronds dancing in the breeze,' Jen recalls. 'As we wandered the rooms, clambering up precipitous ladders and crawling through Wonderland-sized doors, it felt like it might just be the place that would be worth uprooting our lives for.'

With two young children, renovating and decorating their new home is an ongoing challenge. 'When we arrived three years ago on a freezing afternoon in December, we were greeted by a broken oil tank and no hot water, heating or cooker,' says Jen. 'For the first few weeks, we scrambled eggs on the top of the wood burners and all slept together in one bed!'

SHELF LIFE

In the kitchen, open wooden shelving highlights the simple beauty of dried ingredients in attractive storage jars (below). An old wooden storage bench has been used in the dining and living area to display vintage curiosities such as wooden shoe lasts and leather-bound antique books (right). Apples and pears from the garden are harvested and brought indoors (opposite above left and right).

This is a slow and mindful renovation, where great care has been taken to restore Tanyard in a way that is authentic and sympathetic to its rich heritage. Wooden beams have been scrubbed free of orange wax and modern plasterboard/drywall has been removed to allow the wattle and daub to breathe again. Limewash paints from Bauwerk lend a historic feel and beautiful patina to the walls. 'As its custodians for now, our aim is to slowly and sensitively adjust this ancient homestead to make it a soul-warming modern-day home,' says Jen.

Describing her style as 'undone, lived-in and deliberately imperfect', Jen has used a natural palette of tawny golds, browns and creams with accents coming from antique paintings and mirrors, dried flowers and books, artworks and ceramics. Rough walls and scuffed pamments (Norfolk clay floor tiles), scratched floorboards and marked beams are all celebrated for their character.

Seasonal Decor

STAR WREATH

This simple winter wreath decoration was made using an upcycled metal tomato purée/paste tube, a length of wire and a piece of ribbon (left). To create something similar, cut down one side of the tube, then open it out to make a flat sheet of metal. Wash it carefully before using – you could also use foil or a sheet of craft metal instead. Use a craft cutter to make star shapes and pierce a hole in each one using a needle. Thread the stars onto the wire. To make the wreath, twist the wire into overlapping circles. Secure the ends by twisting them together, then add a loop of ribbon and hang up the wreath in your home.

Style Tip

You can easily change the seasonal feel of your home by introducing different colours. In this cosy winter bedroom, pillowcases in dark green and off-white are layered with olive-green linen throws. You don't have to change everything – the ochres of autumn continue here in the curtains and dried flowers.

ADVENTURES IN WONDERLAND

A vintage ladder between two cupboards in the master bedroom climbs up to a hidden chamber (left). From there, an old wooden door leads to a beautiful bathroom under the rafters (opposite). The zinc tub is placed under the window for views of the sky. White-painted floorboards and a dark wall echo the stark contrasts of the winter landscape.

To create a cosy feel, richly coloured long velvet curtains puddle on the wooden floor, vintage hides are draped over armchairs and woollen blankets are piled up on the big sofa.

Upstairs, the vaulted master bedroom is filled with large vintage storage pieces including a huge laundry basket on castors that can be wheeled into place. The bathroom is reached via a painted wooden ladder. At the top, after ducking under a low beam, you enter a soulful space furnished entirely with preloved pieces. A nickel-coated copper bathtub found on eBay sits under a window where you can bathe by candlelight and stargaze as darkness falls. The sink is an old zinc washbasin that was rescued from a neighbour's shed. 'We buy very little new – our bathroom wares come from Mongers of Hingham, wood and other larger pieces from Morways Reclamation and tanks and tubs from JC Gray Antiques & Reclaim, all just up the road,' says Jen. Further afield, other favourite dealers for art, furniture and decorative items include The Textured Room in Sussex, The Old Potato Store in Greater Manchester and Catherine Waters Antiques in Devon.

The family loves to spend time outdoors. In the garden they grow vegetables in vintage galvanized tubs and allow weeds to run wild in the borders. Fennel has self-seeded along the gravel path, its towering seedheads replacing the yellow flowers once summer has passed. Plums, apples and pears are harvested from the trees. 'It was very manicured when we arrived, with clean and tidy beds, tightly pruned roses and a trimmed mulberry tree,' says Jen, 'but it's become wilder with each passing year, which we love.'

Indoors, Tanyard is filled with dried and fresh flowers foraged throughout the year; clay and wooden bowls are filled with dried seedheads, acorns, bleached sea berries and abandoned birds' nests. Old jugs/pitchers and planters overflow with branches from the hedgerow or nearby heath, laden with frothy blossom in summer and richly coloured red berries and evergreen foliage in the winter.

The house itself changes according to the seasons, too. In winter when the light is low, Tanyard's soul sings. The stone fireplaces dance with flames and suppers at the refectory table are enjoyed by candlelight. The family spends evenings watching old films or reading. As they drift off to sleep under layers of blankets, they can hear the sound of screech owls calling into the gloaming and the wind rustling the thatch.

A FOREST CABIN

This cosy black wooden cabin inspired by both Scandinavian and Japanese design can be found on an organic farm in the Netherlands. Inside, owners Leonne and Sander Booman have created a modern yet cocooning and tactile interior. This is Tiny Hotel, a tranquil escape where guests can relax indoors, around the firepit or in the hot tub: the perfect place to winter.

Leonne and Sander have realized their dream of creating a beautiful and natural escape for guests to come and share their passion for nature and a slower pace of life. The three-bedroom cabin, now called the Farm House, is over 20 years old and was an outbuilding on the farm when they arrived. The young couple have spent the past three years renovating the structure, along with a smaller cabin known as the Sheep House. Leonne describes the pair's signature style as 'Japandi with a touch of French cosiness – we love the calm of a minimal interior filled with natural materials.'

The Farm House cabin sits seamlessly within its forest surroundings, as the dark exterior cladding blends into the trees. A wood-fired hot tub and firepit offer a variety of ways to appreciate the picturesque winter landscape while staying warm.

CLEAN LINES

The couple have paid close attention to the use of verticals and horizontals in the space. The painted cladding is a calming backdrop that draws the eye up to the ceiling beams (this page). A rectangular table elongates the dining space (opposite).

ELEMENTS OF STYLE

The materials and colours of winter have been brought indoors in the form of foraged decor and green glassware (left and below left). A wooden storage unit grounds the kitchen area – it makes a useful prep space, but unlike a fixed island it can be easily moved (below). Earthy colours and dark wooden cabinetry are juxtaposed with an oversized white paper lantern and soft pale sheepskins (opposite).

Inside, Leonne and Sander have created a large double-height, open-plan kitchen, dining and living space lined with softly coloured, off-white vertical cladding.

A large sisal rug delineates the living area and offers comfort underfoot; the light filters through sheer linen curtains, which offer privacy and texture. Cosy textiles cover the Scandinavian-style furnishings, which include design classics such as the Hans J Wegner-inspired dining chairs. Wood, wicker, jute, cotton, linen, wool and sheepskins combine to bring comfort and texture to the space.

The bedrooms are decorated in warm blush pinks and terracotta, the beds layered with linen duvets/comforters and woollen blankets. Favourite prints found by the couple in keeping with their Scandinavian style are set against the panelled walls. In the spa-like bathroom, brushed brass fittings and a back-lit mirror warm the cool stone-coloured tiles. Good use has been made of the small space with a wet-room shower and wall-hung WC and vanity, which keep the floor visible and give the illusion of a larger space.

Cuttings from the adjacent forest and foraged finds from local walks are found throughout the cabin – a twisted dried wreath with clouds of dried clematis hung on the wall brings the palette and texture of the winter hedgerows indoors. Fir cones sit in a bowl on the kitchen island, while evergreen fir cuttings in a clay pot can be found on the work surface.

Guests are allowed to fully experience life on the farm, where cows wander past the end of the garden, large rabbits hop around their outdoor enclosure and friendly dogs are frequent visitors. This immersion enhances the connection to nature and wildlife during a stay at Tiny Hotel.

Style Tip

If space is limited, take a leaf out of Leonne's book: swapping bedside tables/nightstands and lamps for wall-mounted versions creates much-needed extra space in a tiny bedroom like this one. Shaker-style peg rails also make a great space-saving alternative to a wardrobe/armoire, especially in a guest room.

CURVE APPEAL

An organic-shaped light (above), pretty half-moon paper bunting and a stool repurposed as a bedside table/nightstand (right) all help soften this space with their gentle curves. A blend of warm pinks alongside icy whites and layered textiles give this cabin the feel of a snug winter hideaway.

The passing of the seasons and an organic lifestyle is integral to Leonne and Sander's design aesthetic and way of life, as their work on the farm is dictated by the hours of sunlight each day. The farm is organic and they try to eat seasonal, local food. The materials they use in their interiors are also kept as raw and authentic as possible, always informed by the natural world around them.

In the warmer months, windows and doors are flung open, meals are taken in the garden and heavy soft furnishings are swapped for light linens and cottons. In winter the cabin becomes a cosy haven; candles lit, soft furnishings plentiful and tactile. The outdoors still plays a central role with walks around the farm, time spent caring for and enjoying the animals and warming up in the hot tub at the end of a working day. 'Our favourite winter activities include sitting in the hot tub surrounded by snow or gathering around the firepit, wrapped in rugs, to enjoy hot chocolate and marshmallows with friends,' says Leonne with a smile.

A door for all Seasons

Enjoy an afternoon collecting and arranging winter greenery to spruce up a porch or doorway. Think beyond the traditional wreaths of the season and create a wild, natural bower that winds its way around the doorway. Keep it simple and rustic, or add large gingham bows, dried flower heads or pomegranates. Use a mix of different textures and shades of green for a more interesting finish. Adding scented bay and eucalyptus foliage also creates a sensory welcome at your door. If you want to augment the scent, you can dip fir cones into essential oils such as rosemary, fir or pine and tie them into your design.

WHAT YOU NEED

Gardening gloves, chicken wire, wire cutters, floristry wire, a hammer, nails, pruning shears and lots of winter foliage (we used rosemary, bay, pine, fir, holly, eucalyptus, olive and myrtle).

1 Wearing gloves, unroll the chicken wire and cut two lengths approximately 30-40cm/12–16in long. Roll each length into a sausage shape and secure the ends with floristry wire. Hammer in nails at the top, middle and bottom of the space you wish to decorate and attach the chicken-wire rolls vertically.

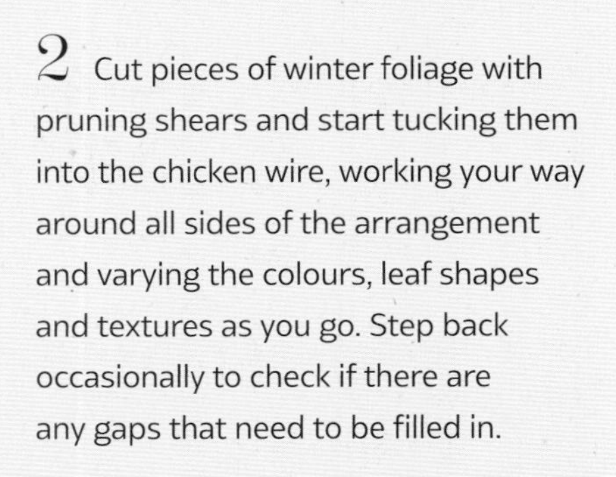

2 Cut pieces of winter foliage with pruning shears and start tucking them into the chicken wire, working your way around all sides of the arrangement and varying the colours, leaf shapes and textures as you go. Step back occasionally to check if there are any gaps that need to be filled in.

3 Continue until there is a nice, full bower and you can no longer see the chicken wire. You can add some additional decorations at this stage according to taste (see introduction above). Top up the foliage as it starts to dry over time, tucking in freshly cut pieces to replenish the display.

Thinking ahead

* Save eucalyptus foliage from winter arrangements and decorations (such as the bower on pages 162–163) and dry it both for reuse and for natural dyeing projects in the spring. You can either hang it to dry in bunches in a cool, dark place or leave with a small amount of water in a vase, where it will dry naturally as the water evaporates.

* Grab your shears and get some fresh air while pruning pear and apple trees and gooseberry and currant bushes. Get rid of any dead wood and crossed stems to give the plants the best chance of an abundant harvest in the year ahead.

* Fill pretty containers with spring bulbs such as daffodils, crocuses, hyacinths and tulips, which can be forced indoors so that they flower in late winter or early spring. Add grit to the potting mix to aid draining and ensure pots are at least 15cm/6in deep for the best results.

A Guide to Seasonal Foliage

What to grow and gather for your home.

Spring

WHAT'S IN FLOWER?

Blossom, hyacinths, muscari, tulips, daffodils, mimosa, lilac, magnolia, alliums, bluebells, cow parsley/Queen Anne's lace, primroses, pussy willow and horse-chestnut trees.

STYLING IDEAS

- Make a joyful spring wreath of sunshine-yellow mimosa to hang at your door (see pages 46–47).
- Arrange branches of flowering blossom in large enamel pitchers.
- Plant terracotta pots with spring bulbs, bringing colour and scent.
- Fill glass vases with plentiful tulips, or place a few individual stems in interesting vintage bottles.
- Place flowering magnolia branches in a vintage glass demijohn.
- Display bunches of narcissi and daffodils in a collection of vintage vases.
- Tie miniature wreaths of spring flowers to chair backs or door handles.
- Collect armfuls of cow parsley/ Queen Anne's lace to fill big enamel pitchers – although you may want to keep these outdoors owing to the flowers' distinctive aroma!
- Gather flowering horse-chestnut branches in jam jars to add a pop of spring green.

GROW YOUR OWN...
WHAT TO DO IN SPRING

- Sow your summer annuals (such as nigella, cosmos, strawflowers, zinnias and sunflowers) to keep on a sunny windowsill.
- Cut mimosa branches and alliums to hang and dry.
- Plant your dahlia tubers now for autumn colour.

Summer

WHAT'S IN FLOWER?

Peonies, roses, foxgloves, daisies, poppies, cornflowers, strawflowers, nigella, hydrangeas, verbena, sea lavender, sea holly, gypsophila, fennel, geraniums, cosmos, sunflowers and sweet peas.

STYLING IDEAS

- Create a floral bower around your door (see pages 90–91).
- Fill pretty jam jars with sweetly scented roses.
- Tie tiny flowers to wicker napkin rings for summer table decorations.
- Make a cloud of gypsophila by pushing stems into a ball of chicken wire and suspending it from the ceiling.
- Decorate your home with large terracotta pots of flowering geraniums.
- Display big bunches of cut sunflowers to brighten a corner.
- Cut blowsy hydrangeas and put in large vases with just a little water (don't top it up), then leave them to dry for year-round use.
- Keep potted herbs on a sunny windowsill for scent and to add to your cooking.
- Place bunches of fragrant sweet peas in bud vases.

GROW YOUR OWN...
WHAT TO DO IN SUMMER

- Prune your fruit trees when the sap is rising in early summer.
- Keep on top of deadheading – many summer flowers will have a second flush if you cut them back after first flowering.
- Cut strawflowers and gypsophila in full flower and hang to dry somewhere cool and dark for enjoying in autumn.

Autumn

WHAT'S IN FLOWER?

Dahlias, chrysanthemums, smoke bush, heather, hops and all kinds of dried flowers, foliage and seedheads that linger at the end of summer: teasel, poppy, bracken, honesty, allium, strawflower, scabious, artichoke and gypsophila.

STYLING IDEAS

- Make a simple wreath of silvery honesty seedheads (see pages 132–133), then save the seeds for spring planting.
- Arrange armfuls of dahlias in zinc buckets or old stone pots to bring rich autumn colour.
- Create a hanging cloud of smoke bush branches over your dining table.
- String up freshly picked hops along a mantelpiece, where they will dry in situ.
- Place a few stems of dried strawflowers in a tiny handmade vase or push them into small holes drilled into a piece of wood.

GROW YOUR OWN...
WHAT TO DO IN AUTUMN

- Plant spring bulbs in the garden or in pots stored in a cool, dark place.
- For midwinter flowering bulbs, plant paperwhite daffodils in vintage containers, then bring them out into the light and warmth indoors a couple of weeks before they are needed.
- Plant tulip bulbs in late autumn, ideally after the first frost.
- If you don't have a smoke bush in your garden, consider planting a sapling now for foliage next year.
- Sow sweet pea seeds ready for flowering next summer.
- Plant *Clematis vitalba* (old man's beard) seeds directly into the soil for flowers next year.
- Now is also the time to plant a eucalyptus tree for abundant foliage next year.

Winter

WHAT'S IN FLOWER?

Paperwhite daffodils, snowdrops, cyclamen and hellebores are some of the few plants in bloom at this time of year. You can also gather pine cones, rosehips and winter foliage: old man's beard, holly, fir, eucalyptus, bay and rosemary.

STYLING IDEAS

- Welcome visitors to your door with an evergreen wreath (see pages 162–163).
- Weave a garland of foliage along your dining table and add a few candles for a cosy glow.
- Fill a large bowl with pine cones to add texture to a tabletop display.
- Tie a bunch of winter greenery with ribbon and use it to decorate an internal door.
- Place a large ceramic planter of moss and berries on a coffee table with some taper candles.
- Display scented flowering bulbs in vintage ceramic or glass vases.
- Twist a slender branch into a simple wreath and cover it with ethereal old man's beard.
- For a statement entrance with a forest feel, create an abundant evergreen bower weaving around a doorway, dotted with seasonal flower heads and scented herbs such as bay and rosemary.

GROW YOUR OWN...
WHAT TO DO IN WINTER

- Plant a fruit tree now for spring blossom next year.
- Choose a pretty spring-flowering tree such as mimosa or lilac to plant in midwinter for spring foliage.
- Plant bare-root roses for flowers next summer.
- Prune mature roses in late winter (after gathering some of the rosehips – leave the rest for the birds) to maximize flowering in summer.

Sources

PAINT

ATELIER ELLIS
ateliерellis.co.uk
Handmade paints in a range of colours inspired by nature.

BAUWERK
bauwerkcolour.com
Modern limewash paints that give a textured, natural look.

CRAIG & ROSE
craigandrose.com
One of the UK's oldest paint manufacturers, founded in 1829.

EDWARD BULMER NATURAL PAINT
edwardbulmerpaint.co.uk
Heritage colours from interior designer Edward Bulmer.

FARROW AND BALL
farrow-ball.com
From subtle neutrals to inky hues, Farrow & Ball's paints are ideal for period homes.

GRAPHENSTONE
graphenstone.co.uk
Made with artisanal lime paste, these paints are eco-friendly and reduce indoor pollution.

INGILBY
ingilby.co.uk
Paints handmade in Suffolk with traditional materials.

KALKLITIR
kalklitir.com
Paint sold in powder form to reduce its eco footprint.

LITTLE GREENE
littlegreene.com
A family-run firm inspired by 300 years of history.

PAINT AND PAPER LIBRARY
paintandpaperlibrary.com
A beautiful palette of 180 hues.

RESSOURCE
ressource-peintures.com
ressourcepaints.us
A French company with a long history of mastering colour.

WALLPAPER

BORÅSTAPETER
borastapeter.com
This Swedish company has produced beautiful wallpapers and fabrics for over a century.

LEWIS & WOOD
lewisandwood.co.uk
Lewis & Wood's wallpapers are united by their individuality and craftsmanship.

SANDERSON
sandersondesigngroup.com
A British brand with patterns dating back to 1860, including collections by William Morris.

TESS NEWALL
tessnewall.com
Wallpapers drawing on historic patterns with an artisanal feel.

FABRICS & TEXTILES

BY MÖLLE
bymolle.com
Fine linen curtains and natural homewares crafted in Europe.

HAINES COLLECTION
hainescollection.co.uk
An edit of surplus designer fabrics and homewares that aims to reduce waste in the interiors industry.

KIRSTEN HECKTERMANN
kirstenhecktermann.com
Kirsten's soft furnishings combine modern and antique textiles with her own hand-dyed fabrics and embroidery.

LIBERTY
libertylondon.com
Beautiful, timeless fabrics from this iconic London company.

LINENME
linenme.com
A wide range of linen home textiles from a family-run business in Lithuania.

MERCHANT AND MILLS
merchantandmills.com
A treasure trove of sewing patterns and fabrics.

PIGLET IN BED
pigletinbed.com
Sustainably sourced linens in a beautiful colour palette.

SLUBBED
slubbedprints.co.uk
Indian block prints, batik and handloom-woven cottons.

THE CLOTH SHOP
theclothshop.net
This London shop specializes in natural and vintage fabrics.

TINSMITHS
tinsmiths.co.uk
Hand-woven and printed textiles, artisanal ceramics, lighting and more.

TILES

BERT & MAY
bertandmay.com
Reclaimed and handmade artisanal tiles in striking patterns and colours.

CA' PIETRA
capietra.com
Curated tile collections from the colour-loving and pattern-heavy to the plain and simple.

CLAYBROOK
claybrookstudio.co.uk
High-quality tiles with a truly eye-catching aesthetic.

FIRED EARTH
firedearth.com
Beautiful encaustic tiles made using natural pigments.

MAITLAND & POATE
maitlandandpoate.com
Reclaimed, antique and handmade tiles from Spain.

OTTO
ottotiles.co.uk
Encaustic cement tiles in Art Deco-influenced patterns.

FURNITURE

ALFRED NEWALL
alfrednewall.com
Wooden pieces made by skilled artisans in the South Downs.

ERCOL
ercol.com
Founded by Lucian Ercolani in 1920, this family-run business sells timeless British furniture.

SEBASTIAN COX
sebastiancox.co.uk
Award-winning bespoke fine furniture.

CERAMICS

CLAIRE HALSEY
IG: @clairebelljar
Stunning handmade lighting, bowls, mugs and vases.

DANTES CERAMICS
dantesceramics.com
Muted, tactile pieces inspired by the Scottish Highlands.

FRANKIE'S STUDIO
frankies.studio
Hand-thrown tableware and accessories in pretty colours.

VINTAGE

AELFRED
aelfred.co.uk
A London warehouse for mid-century Nordic wares.

BAILEYS HOME
baileyshome.com
Modern-rustic furniture, lighting and accessories in rural Herefordshire.

FRENCH ATELIER ANTIQUES
IG: @french_atelier_antiques
Sharon Dallas hosts immersive twice-yearly brocantes at her home in Essex.

IACF
iacf.co.uk
Europe's largest antiques fairs in six UK locations. Get there early for the best finds.

MARLESFORD MILL
IG: @marlesfordmill
A wide range of dealers selling antique and vintage pieces for the home and garden.

MORWAYS RECLAMATION
morways.co.uk
Salvaged building materials from Norfolk and Suffolk.

RAG & BONE
ragandbonebristol.com
A creative collection of vintage furniture, art, collectibles and purely decorative pieces.

REED & SON
reedandson.co.uk
Antiques and secondhand furniture from a family-run business in Essex.

THE BOULE-IN
boule-in.co.uk
Cathy and Peter Bullen's seasonal fêtes bring the feeling of a French market to Bildeston in Suffolk three times a year. You can also shop online all year round.

THE OLD POTATO STORE
theoldpotatostore.co.uk
Antiques, vintage finds and reclaimed salvage sold online from a leafy suburb of Greater Manchester.

TRINOVANTE TRADING
IG: @trinovantetrading
Global antiques, vintage and decorative items.

LIFESTYLE STORES

ANTHROPOLOGIE
anthropologie.com
A place to visit for the creative and artistic visual merchandising in all their stores, as well as for the beautiful homewares from around the world.

JOIN
joinstorelondon.co.uk
Natural, botanical products inspired by the Cornish coast.

RESTE
reste.co.uk
This store in Hastings, East Sussex encourages customers to and live more sustainably.

THE HAMBLEDON
thehambledon.com
This store in Winchester, Hampshire sells a curated range of independent brands from homewares to stationery.

VANIL
vanil.co.uk
Scandinavian-inspired accessories, furniture and home decor.

WATTLE & DAUB
wattleanddaubhome.co.uk
A creative studio and store crafting, sourcing and salvaging objects for the home.

FLOWERS AND PLANTS

BOTANICAL TALES
botanicaltales.com
Floral artist Bex Partridge specializes in 'everlasting' dried flowers, many of which she grows herself in Devon.

BUDS FLOWER SHOP
budsflowershop.co.uk
Fresh and dried flowers beautifully arranged by Amy Giles on the Essex coast.

CHERFOLD FLOWERS
cherfoldflowers.com
Caroline Oleron offers beautiful flower arrangements from her garden studio on the Surrey/ West Sussex border. She also runs seasonal workshops.

JOLLY NICE FARM SHOP
jollynicefarmshop.com
Locally sourced produce from the Cotswolds with a focus on nature-friendly farming.

THE MEADOW PATCH
themeadowpatch.co.uk
A family-run business offering seasonal, sustainable flowers grown and picked by hand in their beautiful meadow in East Anglia.

THE WILD SOCIETY
thewildsociety.co.uk
'Farm to vase' plastic-free British flowers and floral event installations by Alarna McCarry, who grows many of her own flowers and foliage in the Suffolk countryside.

Picture credits

Key: a = above; b = below; l = left; c = centre; r = right.

1 al The family home of digital creator Veronica Lindmark in Sweden @sable_85; 1 ar Styling Kay Prestney & photography Becca Cherry; 1 bl Settle Norfolk, a curated collection of considered stays within a serene parkland settlenorfolk.co.uk @settlenorfolk; 1 br The family home of photographer Tom Bunning and Jen Harrison-Bunning of Slightly Foxed Magazine; 2–5 The home of photographer Mari Magnusson, @anangelinmyhome, marimagnusson.se; 6–7 Ali Allen – Artist and house as location for hire for shoots & workshops; 8 Château de Dirac – photography location; events; rooms; workshops. @lespetitesemplettes @isabelleduboisdumee lespetitesemplettes.com; 9 The home of photographer Mari Magnusson, @anangelinmyhome, marimagnusson.se; 10–11 The location home of interiors blogger, Nat Woods;13 Styling Kay Prestney & photography Becca Cherry; 14–15 Styling & photography by Becca Cherry; 16 above left Styling Kay Prestney & photography Becca Cherry; 16 below Styling & photography by Becca Cherry; 17 Château de Dirac – photography location; events; rooms; workshops. @ lespetitesemplettes @isabelleduboisdumee lespetitesemplettes.com; 18 & 19 al Styling Kay Prestney & photography Becca Cherry; 19 ac & ar Château de Dirac – photography location; events; rooms; workshops. @lespetitesemplettes @isabelleduboisdumee lespetitesemplettes.com; 19 br Styling & photography by Becca Cherry; 20 ar Château de Dirac – photography location; events; rooms; workshops. @lespetitesemplettes @isabelleduboisdumee lespetitesemplettes.com; 20 bl The home of artist Philippa Jeffrey www.philippa-jeffrey.com; 20 br Château de Dirac – photography location; events; rooms; workshops. @lespetitesemplettes @isabelleduboisdumee lespetitesemplettes.com; 21 al & ac Château de Dirac – photography location; events; rooms; workshops. @lespetitesemplettes @isabelleduboisdumee lespetitesemplettes.com; 21 ar & bl The home of artist Philippa Jeffrey www.philippa-jeffrey.com; 21 br The home of photographer Mari Magnusson, @anangelinmyhome, marimagnusson.se; 22 al The home of artist Philippa Jeffrey www.philippa-jeffrey.com; 22 ar Styling Kay Prestney & photography Becca Cherry; 22 br Château de Dirac – photography location; events; rooms; workshops. @lespetitesemplettes @isabelleduboisdumee lespetitesemplettes.com; lespetitesemplettes.com; 23–35 Château de Dirac – photography location; events; rooms; workshops. @lespetitesemplettes @isabelleduboisdumee lespetitesemplettes.com; 36–45 The home of artist Philippa Jeffrey www.philippa-jeffrey.com; 46–47 Styling Kay Prestney & photography Becca Cherry; 48 The home of photographer Mari Magnusson, @anangelinmyhome, marimagnusson.se; 49 a Château de Dirac – photography location; events; rooms; workshops. @ lespetitesemplettes @isabelleduboisdumee lespetitesemplettes.com; 49 b Styling Kay Prestney & photography Becca Cherry; 50–52 l Styling & photography by Becca Cherry; 52 r & 53 The family home of digital creator Veronica Lindmark in Sweden @sable_85; 54 Styling Kay Prestney & photography Becca Cherry; 55 al The home of photographer Mari Magnusson, @anangelinmyhome, marimagnusson.se; 55 ar & b Styling Kay Prestney & photography Becca Cherry; 56 l The location home of interiors blogger, Nat Woods; 56 br The home of photographer Mari Magnusson, @anangelinmyhome, marimagnusson.se; 57 al The home of photographer Mari Magnusson, @anangelinmyhome, marimagnusson.se; 57 ac The location home of interiors blogger, Nat Woods; 57 bl The home of photographer Mari Magnusson, @anangelinmyhome, marimagnusson.se; 57 r The family home of digital creator Veronica Lindmark in Sweden @sable_85; 58 al The family home of digital creator Veronica Lindmark in Sweden @sable_85; 58 bl The location home of interiors blogger, Nat Woods; 58 ar The home of photographer Mari Magnusson, @anangelinmyhome, marimagnusson.se; 59 The location home of interiors blogger, Nat Woods; 60–69 The family home of digital creator Veronica Lindmark in Sweden @sable_85; 70–79 The location home of interiors blogger, Nat Woods; 80–89 The home of photographer Mari Magnusson, @anangelinmyhome, marimagnusson.se; 90–91 Styling Kay Prestney & photography Becca Cherry; 92 The family home of digital creator Veronica Lindmark in Sweden @sable_85; 92 inset Ali Allen – Artist and house as location for hire for shoots & workshops; 93 Styling Kay Prestney & photography Becca Cherry; 94–95 Styling & photography by Becca Cherry; 96 a The home of interior designer Laura Logan @house_of_logan; 96 b Styling & photography by Becca Cherry; 97 Ali Allen – Artist and house as location for hire for shoots & workshops; 98 Styling Kay Prestney & photography Becca Cherry; 99 al Ali Allen – Artist and house as location for hire for shoots & workshops; 99 ac Styling Kay Prestney & photography Becca Cherry; 99 ar & bl Styling & photography by Becca Cherry; 100 a The home of interior designer Laura Logan @house_of_logan; 100 b Ali Allen – Artist and house as location for hire for shoots & workshops; 101 al & inset Ali Allen – Artist and house as location for hire for shoots & workshops; 101 ar Settle Norfolk, a curated collection of considered stays within a serene parkland settlenorfolk.co.uk @settlenorfolk; 101 cl The home of interior designer Laura Logan @house_of_logan; 101 bl & r Settle Norfolk, a curated collection of considered stays within a serene parkland settlenorfolk.co.uk @settlenorfolk; 102 a Ali Allen – Artist and house as location for hire for shoots & workshops; 102 b Settle Norfolk, a curated collection of considered stays

within a serene parkland settlenorfolk.co.uk @settlenorfolk; 103–115 Ali Allen – Artist and house as location for hire for shoots & workshops; 116–123 The home of interior designer Laura Logan @house_of_logan; 124–131 Settle Norfolk, a curated collection of considered stays within a serene parkland settlenorfolk.co.uk @settlenorfolk; 132–133 Styling Kay Prestney & photography Becca Cherry; 134 Settle Norfolk, a curated collection of considered stays within a serene parkland settlenorfolk.co.uk @settlenorfolk; 135 above Settle Norfolk, a curated collection of considered stays within a serene parkland settlenorfolk.co.uk @settlenorfolk; 135 below The location home of interiors blogger, Nat Woods; 136–137 Styling & photography by Becca Cherry; 138 Styling & photography by Becca Cherry; 139 The family home of photographer Tom Bunning and Jen Harrison-Bunning of Slightly Foxed Magazine; 140 Styling Kay Prestney & photography Becca Cherry; 141 a Styling & photography by Becca Cherry; 141 br The family home of photographer Tom Bunning and Jen Harrison-Bunning of Slightly Foxed Magazine; 142 al Ali Allen – Artist and house as location for hire for shoots & workshops; 142 bl The home of photographer Mari Magnusson, @anangelinmyhome, marimagnusson.se; 142 br Styling & photography by Becca Cherry 143 al Tiny-Hotel.nl, designed and owned by Leonne & Sander Booman, available to rent through Airbnb; 143 ar The location home of interiors blogger, Nat Woods; 143 cl Styling Kay Prestney & photography Becca Cherry; 143 bl & br The home of photographer Mari Magnusson, @anangelinmyhome, marimagnusson.se; 144 l The location home of interiors blogger, Nat Woods; 144 r–155 The family home of photographer Tom Bunning and Jen Harrison-Bunning of Slightly Foxed Magazine; 156–161 Tiny-Hotel.nl, designed and owned by Leonne & Sander Booman, available to rent through Airbnb; 162–163 Styling Kay Prestney & photography Becca Cherry; 164 Tiny-Hotel.nl, designed and owned by Leonne & Sander Booman, available to rent through Airbnb; 165–166 Styling & photography by Becca Cherry; 167 l The family home of digital creator Veronica Lindmark in Sweden @sable_85; 167 r Styling & photography by Becca Cherry; 168 The home of interior designer Laura Logan @house_of_logan; 169 l The family home of photographer Tom Bunning and Jen Harrison-Bunning of Slightly Foxed Magazine; 169 r Styling Kay Prestney & photography Becca Cherry; 171 Ali Allen – Artist and house as location for hire for shoots & workshops; 173 The home of artist Philippa Jeffrey www.philippa-jeffrey.com; 176 Ali Allen – Artist and house as location for hire for shoots & workshops.

The publisher would also like to thank Claire Halsey of @clairebelljar, Jill & Christopher Hamblin and Beckie Batchelor of @themakingbee for the use of their homes for photography.

Business credits

ALI ALLEN
House as location for hire for shoots & workshops
E: ali@aliallen.co.uk
www.aliallen.co.uk
6–7; 92 inset; 97; 99 al; 100 b; 101 al; 101 inset; 102 a; 103; 104–115; 142 al; 171; 176.

LAURA LOGAN
Interior Designer
@house_of_logan
and
Architect: EJ Studio
28 Contemporis
Bristol BS8 4HB
lizzie@ejstudio.co.uk
www.ejstudio.co.uk
and
Joinery: Tim Gaudin
gaudin.carpentry@gmail.com
www.timgaudin.com
96 a; 100 a; 101 cl; 116–123; 168.

TOM BUNNING
www.tombunning.com
JEN HARRISON-BUNNING
www.foxedquarterly.com
1 br; 139; 141 br; 144 r–155; 169 l.

TINY HOTEL
Leonne & Sander Booman
Heibloem 11
5388 VV Nistelrode
The Netherlands
info@tiny-hotel.nl
www.tiny-hotel.nl
@tinyhotel_nl
143 al; 156–161; 164.

CHÂTEAU DE DIRAC
16410 Dirac, France
Photography location; events; rooms; workshops.
@chateaudedirac
@lespetitesemplettes
www.lespetitesemplettes.com
Isabelle Dubois-Dumée
@isabelleduboisdumee
8; 17; 19 ac; 20 ar; 20 br; 21 al; 21 ac; 22 br; 23–35; 49 a.

MARI MAGNUSSON
Photographer
@anangelinmyhome
www.marimagnusson.se
2–5; 9; 21 br; 48; 55 al; 56 br; 57 al; 57 bl; 58 ar; 80–89; 142 bl; 143 bl; 143 br.

NATALIE WOODS
Interiors Blogger
House available to hire through @laid_back_farmhouse
10–11; 56 l; 57 ac; 58 bl; 59; 70–79; 135 b; 143 ar; 144 l.

PHILIPPA JEFFREY
Artist
www.philippa-jeffrey.com
20 bl; 21 ar; 21 bl; 22 al; 36–45; 173.

VERONICA LINDMARK
Digital Creator
@Sable_85
1 al; 52 r; 53; 57 r; 58 al; 60–69; 92; 167 l.

SETTLE NORFOLK
Shropham
Norfolk NR17 1EA
+44 (0) 1953 497030
hello@settlenorfolk.co.uk
settlenorfolk.co.uk
@settlenorfolk
1 bl; 101 ar; 101 bl; 101 r; 102 b; 124–131; 134; 135 a.

Index

Projects are in *italics*

Thank you

This book is dedicated to our children Bella and Finn, Leila and Jasper, in the hope that they (and future generations) value our beautiful planet and enjoy the mental and physical benefits of a life lived in close connection to the seasons.

Thank you to Andy and Adam for all their support and for holding the fort in our absence on our book-writing travels.

A huge thank you to our publisher Ryland Peters & Small for giving us the opportunity to realize our dream of creating a book.

Special thanks to Jess Walton, location researcher, for helping us to find the beautiful homes we have featured in our book and for her patience weaving shoot travels and logistics across the UK, Sweden, France and the Netherlands around our work commitments and family lives.

Thank you to Annabel Morgan, senior commissioning editor, and Leslie Harrington, creative director, for believing in our vision of sharing the benefits of seasonal living in a beautiful interiors book. To Patricia Harrington, head of production, for her work alongside the printers ensuring that our book has a beautiful, tactile and timeless physical format.

A huge thank you to the brilliant Megan Smith, senior designer, for her creative talents and endless patience across emails, international Zoom calls and telephone conversations as she took all our images and ideas and waved her magic wand to turn them into beautifully designed and laid out pages. A big thank you to our talented editor Sophie Devlin for her patient guidance on how to write a book and for editing our lengthy copy into the required word count and format.

Lastly, and most importantly, such a very heartfelt thank you to all the wonderful homeowners who, without exception, were so incredibly kind, generous and welcoming. We have been so inspired by your creative talents and overwhelmed by your hospitality and enthusiasm for our project. We feel lucky to call you our friends and so enjoyed our time together. With the exception of our late-night tour of every EV charging point in Turnhout on the Belgian/Dutch border, we wish we could do it all again!

Kay and Becca
X